W9-BEA-624

On Kissing, Tickling, and Being Bored

On Kissing, Tickling, and Being Bored

Psychoanalytic Essays on the Unexamined Life

ADAM PHILLIPS

HARVARD UNIVERSITY PRESS
Cambridge, Massachusetts

Copyright © 1993 by Adam Phillips
All rights reserved
Printed in the United States of America
10 9 8 7 6 5 4 3 2

This book is printed on acid-free paper, and its binding materials have been chosen for strength and durability.

Library of Congress Cataloging-in-Publication Data

Phillips, Adam.
    On kissing, tickling, and being bored: psychoanalytic essays on
the unexamined life / Adam Phillips.
        p.   cm.
    Includes index.
    ISBN 0–674–63462–4 (alk. paper)
    1. Psychoanalysis.   2. Freud, Sigmund, 1856–1939.   3. Winnicott,
D. W. (Donald Woods), 1896–1971.   I. Title.
RC509.P55   1993
616.89′17—dc20   92–20662
                                                                              CIP

For Hugh Haughton

Preface

Because psychoanalysis is about the most ordinary things in the world it should not be difficult to be interested in. The essays in this book have been written in the belief that any psychoanalytic theory that is of interest only to members of the profession is unlikely to be worth reading. So I am grateful to have been able to publish most of them originally in journals—the *Nouvelle Revue de Psychanalyse, Raritan,* the *London Review of Books*—which have, as it were, a wider appeal. Each of these journals, in quite different ways, endorses J. L. Austin's remark that "it is not enough to show how clever we are by showing how obscure everything is." It was at the invitation of Michel Gribinski and J.-B. Pontalis, the editors of the *Nouvelle Revue,* that I first began writing the essays in this book. I have gained a great deal from their incitement, their translations, and their hospitality (and the fact that they are unbeglamored by obscurity). Similarly, in Richard Poirier and Suzanne Hyman at *Raritan* and Mary-Kay Wilmers at the *London Review of Books,* I have had the kind of congenial and attentive editors that have improved everything that I have submitted to them. Also, at Harvard University Press I am very grateful to Angela von der Lippe and Lindsay Waters for keeping faith with the project over several years, and to Ann Hawthorne for editing the manuscript with such a good ear.

Jacqueline Rose made enormous differences at the last moment; the book has been braced by her shrewd enthusiasm. In our clinical work with children and families at Charing Cross Hospital, my colleague Glenda Fredman has transformed the way I think about psychoanalysis; some of these essays derive from conversations we have had, and some of the best lines in them may be hers. Sarah Spankie has entitled more than this particular book.

Throughout the text, I have observed the economical but obviously unsatisfactory convention of using the masculine pronoun.

Contents

Introduction   1

1. On Tickling   9

2. First Hates: Phobias in Theory   12

3. On Risk and Solitude   27

4. On Composure   42

5. Worrying and Its Discontents   47

6. Returning the Dream:
   In Memoriam Masud Khan   59

7. On Being Bored   68

8. Looking at Obstacles   79

9. Plotting for Kisses   93

10. Playing Mothers: Between Pedagogy
    and Transference   101

11. Psychoanalysis and Idolatry   109

   Notes   123

   Credits   130

   Index   131

The results of life are uncalculated and uncalculable. The years teach much which the days never know. The persons who compose our company converse, and come and go, and design and execute many things, and somewhat comes of it all, but an unlooked-for result. The individual is always mistaken. He designed many things, and drew in other persons as coadjutors, quarrelled with some or all, blundered much, and something is done; all are a little advanced, but the individual is always mistaken. It turns out somewhat new and very unlike what he promised himself.

Ralph Waldo Emerson, *Experience*

Which is wrong? The weather or our calendars?

John Cage, *A Year from Monday*

When people think they've seen enough of something, but there's more, and no change of shot, then they react in a curiously livid way.

Wim Wenders, *Time Sequences, Continuity of Movement*

Introduction

Brichard was quite right when he said to me with his
usual malice: "When you're in love with a woman, you
must ask yourself: What do I want to do with her?"

Stendhal, *The Life of Henry Brulard*

When Freud began to discover what we now think of as
psychoanalysis, it was clear to him what it was to be used for.
It was a new method, a potential form of cure, in the medical
treatment of what were then called hysterical symptoms. And
insofar as psychoanalysis was a medical treatment, the concept
of cure seemed relatively unproblematic. "I have often in my
own mind," Freud wrote,

> compared cathartic psychotherapy with surgical inter-
> vention. I have described my treatments as psychothera-
> peutic operations; and I have brought out their analogy
> with the opening up of a cavity filled with pus, the scrap-
> ing out of a carious region, etc. An analogy of this kind
> finds its justification not so much in the removal of what
> is pathological as in the establishment of conditions that
> are more likely to lead the course of the process in the
> direction of recovery.[1]

In this concluding section of *Studies on Hysteria* (1895),
Freud is interested in the consequences of his analogy. He is
comparing talking to someone with a surgical operation, which
now seems an unusual thing to do (for obvious reasons, sur-
geons don't tend to think of their work as a form of conversation). The operation, Freud suggests, is not the cure; it is only
the prelude to the cure. By removing the pathological material
the surgeon creates the conditions in which the cure can take

place. The cure can begin only after the treatment has ended. The psychotherapist simply clears the way to establish the conditions requisite for recovery. Obstacles are removed to facilitate a possible process. But to believe in such a process, and to know what a cure is—what recovery looks like—the doctor must already know what a life is supposed to look like. In any analogy—and Freud had to be preoccupied with analogies for psychoanalysis because it was so difficult to place—two sets of largely tacit assumptions seem to join forces.

All of Freud's by now well-known analogies for the skill of the psychoanalyst are in one sense immensely reassuring. They orientate the curious very quickly. The detective knows a clue when he sees one, and has a recondite ability to read it; the archaeologist can imagine a past that makes sense of the rubble; and the doctor, of course, recognizes the symptoms of a disease. In each of these professions the pragmatic aims of their respective practices are apparently clear. All of these professions can formulate their aims because they have them (or vice versa). The vocabularies that constitute their practices are their idea of what they are attempting to do. And because their tasks are definable—and teachable—they will know what it is to fail. In other words, canonical texts, persuasive practitioners, and training institutions conspire to create the necessary aura of plausibility. Even if there are mavericks like Sherlock Holmes, they can be mavericks only against a backdrop of orthodoxy.

Psychoanalysis, at its inception, had no texts, no institutions, and no rhetoric; all it had to see itself with were analogies with other forms of practice. The first practitioners of psychoanalysis were making it up as they went along, Freud being the prototype of the "wild analyst." Psychoanalysis, that is to say, was improvised; but improvised, despite the medical training of the early analysts, out of a peculiarly indefinable set of conventions. Freud had to improvise between the available analogies, and he took them, sometimes in spite of himself, from the sciences and the arts. Something new, after all, can be compared only with something from the past, something already established. Even though Freud's analogies were compelling, sustaining at once the romance and the worthiness of psychoanalysis, he was unwilling to describe the ways in which psychoanalysis was *unlike* the professions he most admired; the ways in which psychoanalysis, for example—as I suggest at various points in these essays—turns the familiar concept of cure into the problem rather than the solution. It is indeed disappointing—as I show in "Playing Mothers"—that after Freud had invented a new kind of person called a psychoanalyst, some clinicians began to believe that a psychoanalyst should be, in some way, "like" a mother. Psychoanalysts have been tardy about this problem of unlikeness.

Psychoanalysis began, then, as a kind of virtuoso improvisation within the science of medicine; and free association—the heart of psychoanalytic treatment—is itself ritualized improvisation. But Freud was determined to keep psychoanalysis officially in the realm of scientific rigor, partly, I think, because improvisation is difficult to legitimate—and to sell—outside of a cult of genius. With the invention of psychoanalysis—or rather, with the discovery of what he called the unconscious—Freud glimpsed a daunting prospect: a profession of improvisers. And in the ethos of Freud and his followers, improvisation was closer to the inspiration of artists than to the discipline of scientists. Prospectively, and despite the range of his own cultural interests, Freud wanted to think of himself as a scientist. Retrospectively it seems rather as though it was very much the confluence of disparate traditions—and traditionally separated disciplines—that produced the new sentences that are called psychoanalytic theory. Curiosity, which Freud did so much to redescribe, is always opportunism.

One does not need to idealize either the indefinite or the improvised to think that the fact that psychoanalysis is difficult to place—unlike a lot of things to which it is similar—may be one of its distinctive virtues. Nor need it be cause for dismay—despite the splits and the synthesizing of theories (the having of "dialogues") in contemporary psychoanalysis—that psychoanalysis can be a circus with many acts. There is no reason why psychoanalysts should agree with one another—be either zealously partisan or gently pluralist—nor is there any reason to believe that if the perfect synthesis of competing theories is achieved it will speak inside the analyst like a god telling him what to do in the ordinary disarray of a psychoanalytic session. A repertoire might be more useful than a conviction; especially if one wants to keep in mind that there are many kinds of good life.

The psychoanalysis that interests me—and that is entertained in these essays—tries to do this. It is prodigal in its use of analogy and promiscuous in its references because the very process of comparing and contrasting, mixing and matching, offers the possibility of more enlivening and diverse redescriptions. One sense in which a life is always unexamined—or endlessly examinable—is that it can always be described in different ways, from different points of view. And psychoanalysis can be good at showing the ways in which certain points of view become invested with authority; but it is also too good at assuming an authoritative point of view for itself. By pooling the language of psychoanalysis rather than hoarding it—by circulating it in unusual places with other languages—psychoanalysis can be relieved of the knowingness that makes it look silly; the knowingness that comes from its "splendid isolation," the fantasies of inner superiority in the profession. And it keeps alive the potentially glib irony that psychoanalysts are experts—if they are experts about anything—about the fact that there are no experts on life. Psychoanalysis is a story—and a way of telling stories—that makes some people feel better. But there are, and have been, many stories in the culture and in other cultures through which people examine, and do other things to, their lives. Psychoanalysis—as a form of conversation—is worth having only if it makes our lives more interesting, or funnier, or sadder, or more tormented, or whatever it is about ourselves that we value and want to promote; and especially if it helps us find new things about ourselves that we didn't know we could value. New virtues are surprisingly rare.

As an evolving and relatively new story it is one of the distinctive virtues of psychoanalysis that it can give us new lines on things that matter to us (like kissing, tickling, and being bored). But psychoanalysis itself has now become available as an analogy, and analogies, of course, work both ways. If psychoanalysis can make worrying more interesting, then worrying can make psychoanalysis more interesting. It is this kind of enthusiasm that psychoanalysis is particularly prone to—significantly so—and that Freud tried to use the idea of science to manage, to keep the traffic going one way. When he did so in, for example, "The Question of Weltanschauung" in *The New Introductory Lectures,* he became unusually strident in his dismissals of philosophy, art, and religion, producing caricatures of them in his promotion of science as the supreme method of human inquiry. Science, and psychoanalysis as a science, can be used to explain religion, but religion cannot—indeed must not—be used to explain science. Science, as I show in "Psychoanalysis and Idolatry," becomes for Freud the method he believes to be most exempt from wishfulness, and therefore the most truthful (and despite the fact that the relationship to truth becomes a sadomasochistic one, truth being that which it is better for us to submit to). Having, through psychoanalysis, placed the wish at the center of mental life, the wish then becomes the saboteur, the contaminator, of truth.

By allying psychoanalysis so insistently with science—with a pursuit of truth irrespective of value—it was as though Freud could also exempt himself and his "new science" from the old question of what a good life is. But his fear of wishing and his disavowal of psychoanalysis as a form of ethical inquiry are, of course, connected; because another version of the question, What constitutes a good life? is the question, What kind of person does one want to be? Quite understandably this has been a question—and a connection—that Freud, and psychoanalysts after him, have been wary of. It is, after all, an extraordinary thing to take wishing seriously. If it were to be taken seriously in psychoanalytic trainings, for example, the question for the trainee at any given moment would not be, Am I doing this properly? but, Do I want to be the kind of person, say, who at this moment refuses to answer the patient's question?

Insofar as psychoanalysis is essentialist—when, for example, psychoanalysts claim to believe in instincts, development, or innate preconceptions—it can only try to reconcile people to who they are by telling them what that is. In Freud's work, as we know, there is an inspiring contradiction: on the one hand he describes what a life is, a developmental progress through the oral, anal, and phallic stages fueled by the "war" between two fundamental instincts, Eros and Thanatos; and on the other hand he describes an unconscious that is by definition the saboteur of intelligibility and normative life-stories. Indeed psychoanalysis, as described by Freud, might make us wonder why it is so difficult to imagine a life *without* normative life-stories. A good life, in this context, is either the successful negotiation of a more or less preset developmental project (in which the question, Set by whom? might seem irrelevant); or it can be something that we make up as we go along, according to our wishes, in endlessly proliferating and competing versions, the unconscious, as Richard Rorty has remarked, feeding us our best lines.[2] Psychoanalysis in this version cannot help people, because there is nothing wrong with anybody; it can only engage them in useful and interesting conversations. So one could then say that as a form of treatment psychoanalysis is a conversation that enables people to understand what stops them from having the kinds of conversation they want, and how they have come to believe that these particular conversations are worth wanting. Rather than: psychoanalysis is a conversation that helps people get back on track. Psychoanalysis, in other words, would be a curiosity profession instead of a helping profession. It is, of course, one of the tacit assumptions of psychoanalysis that there can be no good life, and no curiosity, without talking.

Psychoanalysis does not assume, in the same way, the value of writing (one couldn't do analysis as a correspondence course, although some accounts of analysis sound remarkably like one). But the kind of distinction I have been making for the treatment of psychoanalysis also holds for the writing of psychoanalysis. One of the dramas that these essays try to sustain—and that is present in every clinical encounter—is the antagonism between the already narrated, examined life of developmental theory and the always potential life implied by the idea of the unconscious. The conflict between knowing what a life is and the sense that a life contains within it something that makes such knowing impossible is at the heart of Freud's enterprise. So in one kind of psychoanalytic writing the theorist will be telling us by virtue of his knowledge of development or the contents of the internal world what a life should be like, however tentatively this may be put. And in another kind of psychoanalytic writing—which in its most extreme and sometimes inspired form pretends to ape the idea of the unconscious—there is a different kind of conscious wish at work: rather than informing the reader there is an attempt, to echo Emerson, to return the reader to his own thoughts whatever their majesty, to evoke by provocation. According to this way of doing it, thoroughness is not inciting. No amount of "evidence" or research will convince the un-amused that a joke is funny. And by the same token ambiguity, inconsistency, or sentences that make you wonder whether the writer really knows what he is talking about, are considered to be no bad thing. I prefer—and write in these essays—this kind of psychoanalysis, but each is impossible without the other. Their complicity is traditionally underrated in psychoanalysis. One can put the whole notion of what it is to understand into question—as psychoanalysis does—without sneering at the wish for intelligibility, the wish to find stories for whatever is unbecoming.

The different kinds of psychoanalysis have different proj-ects, different "dreams of Eden," to use Auden's phrase.[3] So we don't have to worry, for example, about whether psycho-analysis is scientific or not; we simply have to ask what we want to do with it. People have traditionally come for psychoanalytic conversation because the story they are telling themselves about their lives has stopped, or become too painful, or both. The aim of the analysis is to restore the loose ends—and the looser beginnings—to the story. But if the story is fixed—if the patient ends up speaking psychoanalysis—we must assume that something has been lost in translation. Psychoanalysis is essentially a transitional language, one possible bridge to a more personal, less compliant idiom. It is useful only as a contribution to forms of local knowledge, as one among the many language games in a culture (and the local, of course, starts with the individual person and his always recondite sense of himself). In order to regain interest in the idea of the unconscious we have to lose interest in the idea of the superordinate point of view:

> Who has once met
> irony will burst into laughter
> during the prophet's lecture.[4]

- 1 -

On Tickling

The ear says more
Than any tongue.

W. S. Graham, "The Hill of Intrusion"

"If you tickle us, do we not laugh?" asks Shylock, defining himself as human as he begins to "feed" his revenge. And what is more ordinary in the child's life than his hunger for revenge and, indeed, the experience of being tickled? From a psychoanalytic point of view it is curious that this common, perhaps universal, experience has rarely been thought about; and not surprising that once we look at it we can see so much.

An absolute of calculation and innocence, the adult's tickling of the child is an obviously acceptable form of sensuous excitement between parents and children in the family. The child who will be able to feed himself, the child who will masturbate, will never be able to tickle himself. It is the pleasure he cannot reproduce in the absence of the other. "From the fact that a child can hardly tickle itself," Darwin wrote in his *Expression of the Emotions in Man and Animals,* "or in a much less degree than when tickled by another person, it seems that the precise point to be touched must not be known." An enigmatic conclusion, which, though manifestly untrue—children know exactly, like adults, where they are ticklish—alerts us to the fact that these "precise points" are a kind of useless knowledge to the child, that they matter only as shared knowledge. They require the enacted recognition of the other.

Helpless with pleasure, and usually inviting this helplessness, the child, in the ordinary, affectionate, perverse scenario of being tickled, is wholly exploitable. Specific adults know where the child is ticklish—it is, of course, only too easy to find out—but it is always idiosyncratic, a piece of personal history, and rarely what Freud called one of the "predestined erotogenic zones." Through tickling, the child will be initiated in a distinctive way into the helplessness and disarray of a certain primitive kind of pleasure, dependent on the adult to hold[1] and not to exploit the experience. And this means to stop at the blurred point, so acutely felt in tickling, at which pleasure becomes pain, and the child experiences an intensely anguished confusion; because the tickling narrative, unlike the sexual narrative, has no climax. It has to stop, or the real humiliation begins. The child, as the mother says, will get hysterical.

In English, the meaning of the word *tickle* is, so to speak, almost antithetical, employing, as Freud said of the dreamwork, "the same means of representation for expressing contraries." The *Oxford English Dictionary* cites, among nineteen definitions of the word, the following: "In unstable equilibrium, easily upset or overthrown, insecure, tottering, crazy . . . nicely poised." Other definitions describe a range of experience from excessive credulity to incontinence. The word speaks of the precarious, and so of the erotic. To tickle is, above all, to seduce, often by amusement. But of the two references to tickling in Freud (both in the *Three Essays on the Theory of Sexuality*), it is used as virtually synonymous with stroking: included, quite accurately and unobtrusively, as part of the child's ordinary sensuous life. Describing the characteristics of an erotogenic zone, Freud writes:

> It is part of the skin or mucous membrane in which stimuli of a certain sort evoke a feeling of pleasure possessing a particular quality. There can be no doubt that the stimuli which produce the pleasure are governed by special conditions, though we do not know what those are. A rhythmic character must play a part among them and the analogy of tickling is forced upon our notice. It seems less certain whether the character of the pleasurable feeling evoked by the stimulus should be described as a

"specific" one—a "specific" quality in which the sexual factor would precisely lie. Psychology is still so much in the dark in questions of pleasure and unpleasure that the most cautious assumption is the one most to be recommended.[2]

Freud is certain here only of what he does not know. But in the light of his uncertainty, which provokes the most careful questions, what is the most cautious assumption we can make about these specific pleasures called tickling and being tickled? In the elaborate repertoire of intrusions, what is the quality—that is to say, the fantasy—of the experience? Certainly there is no immediate pressing biological need in this intent, often frenetic contact that so quickly reinstates a distance, only equally quickly to create another invitation. Is the tickling scene, at its most reassuring, not a unique representation of the over-displacement of desire and, at its most unsettling, a paradigm of the perverse contract? Does it not highlight, this delightful game, the impossibility of satisfaction and of reunion, with its continual reenactment of the irresistible attraction and the inevitable repulsion of the object, in which the final satisfaction is frustration?

A girl of eight who keeps "losing her stories" in the session because she has too much to say, who cannot keep still for a moment, suddenly interrupts herself by saying to me, "I can only think of you when I don't think of you." This same, endlessly elusive child—elusiveness, that is, the inverse of obsessionality—ends a session telling me, "When we play monsters, and mummy catches me, she never kills me, she only tickles me!"

"We can cause laughing by tickling the skin," Darwin noted of the only sensuous contact that makes one laugh. An extraordinary fact condensing so much of psychoanalytic interest, but one of which so little is spoken. Perhaps in the cumulative trauma that is development we have had the experience but deferred the meaning.

- 2 -

First Hates:
Phobias in Theory

His radical solutions were rendered vain by the conventionality of his problems.

George Santayana, *My Host the World*

In his chapter "Instinct" in *Psychology: The Briefer Course* (1892), William James writes:

> The progress from brute to man is characterised by nothing so much as by the decrease in frequency of proper occasions for fear. In civilised life, in particular, it has at last become possible for large numbers of people to pass from the cradle to the grave without ever having had a pang of genuine fear. Many of us need an attack of mental disease to teach us the meaning of the word. Hence the possibility of so much blindly optimistic philosophy and religion.[1]

James, of course, is always looking for good transitions, for the passages that work for us. Like Freud, but for different reasons, he is wary of the progress in civilized life. For Freud, civilization compromises our desire; for James here, it compromises our fear. If civilization protects us, or overprotects us, the absence of danger can make us unrealistic. We may need an attack of mental disease as the only available reminder of "proper occasions for fear." Without proper occasions we lose the meaning of an important word. This mental disease that James recommends, partly from his own experience, or rather the real fear that it entails, should temper speculation, setting limits to the naive ambitions of metaphysics.

But fear, especially at its most irrational, perplexes James in an interesting way; it connects for him three of his most consistent preoccupations: blindness, optimism, and the doing of philosophy. Because, unlike Freud, he doesn't see fear and desire as inextricable, he is more openly puzzled. Even though "a certain amount of timidity obviously adapts us to the world we live in," he writes, "the fear paroxysm is surely altogether harmful to him who is its prey." After considering the virtues of immobility—the insane and the terrified "feel safer and more comfortable" in their "statue-like, crouching immobility"—James refers at the very end of his chapter on fear to "the strange symptom which has been described of late years by the rather absurd name of agoraphobia." After describing the symptoms, which "have no utility in a civilised man," he manages to make sense of this puzzling new phenomenon only by comparing it to the way in which both domestic cats and many small wild animals approach large open spaces. "When we see this," he writes,

> we are strongly tempted to ask whether such an odd kind
> of fear in us be not due to the accidental resurrection,
> through disease, of a sort of instinct which may in some
> of our more remote ancestors have had a permanent and
> on the whole a useful part to play.[2]

The "disease" returns the patient to his instinctual heritage; but this heritage is now redundant because, in actuality, there is nothing to fear. Agoraphobics, James suggests, are living in the past, the evolutionary past ("the ordinary cock-sure evolutionist," James remarks in his droll way, "ought to have no difficulty in explaining these terrors").[3] The agoraphobic is, as it were, speaking a dead language. So to understand agoraphobia in James's terms, we have to recontextualize the fear, put it back in its proper place, or rather, time. There is nothing really irrational about phobic terror; it is an accurate recognition of something, something that Darwinian evolution can supply a picture for. Fear itself cannot be wrong, even if it is difficult to find out where it fits.

A phobia nevertheless is, perhaps in both senses, an improper occasion for fear, an enforced suspension of disbelief.

James's description of the agoraphobic patient "seized with pal-
pitation and terror at the sight of any open place or broad street
which he has to cross alone" is a vivid picture of a phobia as
an impossible transition. And it can be linked—as a kind of
cartoon—with one of James's famous notions of truth; the
agoraphobic becoming, as it were, the compulsive saboteur of
some of his own truth. "Pragmatism gets her general notion of
truth," James writes in his book of that title,

> as something essentially bound up with the way in which
> one moment in our experience may lead us towards other
> moments which it will be worth while to have been led
> to. Primarily, and on the common-sense level, the truth
> of a state of mind means this function of *a leading that is
> worth while*.[4]

The agoraphobic is the figure of the compromised prag-
matist. The threshold of experience between this one moment
and the next is aversive. He wants to go somewhere—or, in
James's more suggestive terms, be led somewhere—but he is
unable to find out whether it is as worthwhile (in both senses)
as he thinks. The terror, or the inability to hold the terror,
preempts possible future states of mind, and so precludes their
evaluation. A phobia, in other words, protects a person from
his own curiosity.

"Agoraphobia," Freud wrote in a letter to Wilhelm Fliess
in 1887, "seems to depend on a romance of prostitution."
Despite James's misgiving about its "rather absurd name," and
despite its being Greeked for prestigious legitimation, agoraphobia seems rather nicely named. The agora, after all, was
that ancient place where words and goods and money were
exchanged. Confronted with an open space, as James and Freud
both agree, the agoraphobic fears that something nasty is going
to be exchanged: one state of mind for another, one desire for
another. But the phobia ensures a repression of opportunity, a
foreclosing of the possibilities for exchange ("a projection is
dangerous," the psychoanalyst André Green has written, "when
it prevents the simultaneous formation of an introjection"; in a
phobia one is literally unable to take in what one has invented).

The agoraphobic, that is to say, knows—Freud would say unconsciously—what the space is for, or what he wants to use it for. It then ceases, as though by magic, to be an open space, or what James calls a pluralistic universe.[5] It simply leads into the past, into the old world.

James and Freud use explanation in quite different ways. For James the question is not so much, Is it true? as How would my life be better if I believed it? For Freud the first question— the unconscious question, so to speak—is, What do I want? and then, What fantasies of truth do I need to legitimate it? But because for James there can never be any knowing beforehand, he cannot presume to universalize his conclusions. And this is because there is no end to them; in this sense he is a freer associationist than Freud. "It is enough to ask of each of us," he concludes in his great talk "On a Certain Blindness in Human Beings," "that he should be faithful to his own opportunities and make the most of his own blessings, without presuming to regulate the rest of the vast field."[6] The risk for the phobic person, as for the psychoanalyst, is that he has already used his explanations to delimit his opportunities.

> . . . a face which inspires fear or delight (the object of fear or delight) is not on that account its cause, but—one might say—its target.
>
> Ludwig Wittgenstein, *Philosophical Investigations*

The question of where the fear belongs—or what it is worthwhile to fear—is one that occupies both the phobic person and his interpreter. Freud himself at one point speculated that childhood phobias of small animals and thunder could be "the atrophied remainders of congenital preparation for real dangers that are so clearly developed in other animals."[7] If Freud and James agree here, with Darwinian common sense, that phobias are derivative forms of self-protection, that phobic terror is irrational only insofar as it has missed its target, they radically disagree about what there is to fear and where it comes from. They fill the agoraphobic space—its empty page, so to speak— in quite different ways.

James's open space, for the agoraphobic, evokes phylo-genetic memory; Freud's open space evokes personal memory (and memory for Freud is always of desire and the parented past). James's open space may be full of potential predators, but in Freud's open space a person may turn into a predator. "The anxiety felt in agoraphobia," Freud writes in 1926,

> (a subject that has been less thoroughly studied) seems to be the ego's fear of sexual temptation—a fear which, after all, must be connected in its origins with the fear of castration. As far as can be seen at present, the majority of phobias go back to an anxiety of this kind felt by the ego in regard to the demands of the libido.[8]

For the agoraphobic the open space represents the setting for a possible incestuous sexual encounter punishable by castra-tion. Because sexuality begins in incestuous fantasy, it always smacks of the forbidden. So the phobic scenario, in Freud's view, appears to invite an illicit reenactment from the past, a place where, quite unwittingly, a memory could be cast. For the agoraphobic to go out is to give the past a future, to bring it forward, so to speak. What the phobic fears, unconsciously, is not only the replication of this truant past, but also its mod-ification in ways that cannot be anticipated. If one loses the replica, one might lose the original. These phobic scenarios are like antiepiphanies in which memory, rather than being released into images and atmospheres, is frozen into terror. Whereas the epiphany, in the Proustian sense, is contingent and surprising, the phobia is reliable. The phobia, which hoards the past, can be the one place in a person's life where meaning apparently never changes; but this depends upon one's never knowing what the meaning is.

Given the insistence and the mobility of the libido in Freud's account, any occasion might be a proper occasion for fear. Desire—or what we can, in a different language, call parts of the self—insofar as it is experienced as intolerable has to be put somewhere else, projected into hiding. There it can be acknowledged in terror, but never known about. The profoundest way of recognizing something, or the only way of recognizing some things, Freud will imply, is through hiding them from oneself. And what is profound, or rather of interest, is not only what one has hidden but also the ways one has of hiding it. We know only, of course—as in a phobia—about the repressions that break down. So it is as though, from a psychoanalytic point of view, our unbearable self-knowledge leads a secret life; as though there is self-knowledge, but not for us. For Freud, what has to be explained is not why someone is phobic, but how anyone ever stops being anything other than phobic.

> A "no" from a person in analysis is quite as ambiguous as a "yes."
>
> Sigmund Freud, *Constructions in Analysis*

An acutely claustrophobic man in his early forties—although his phobia has increasingly focused on the theater, which he has always "loved"—remembers, in an otherwise desultory session, a childhood memory. At about age eight he goes to the oculist, and one of the tests he is made to do "to find out about his coordination" is to look down something like a telescope and with his hands put the dog he sees into the cage that he sees. He does it successfully and with real pleasure; and the oculist, a "benign man," says to him, "Well, you'll never be able to join the RAF!" Understanding that he will never be able to be a pilot, he is "shattered," "although until that moment it had never occurred to me that I wanted to." And then he adds, sarcastically, that as an adult he has always been really excited about traveling in airplanes. It is clear to both of us that this is something of an ambiguous triumph.

I remind him that his terror in the theater—the fantasy he desperately wards off, and so "sees" instead of the play—is that he will jump off the balcony (he had confessed to me in our first meeting, with some satisfaction, that he always sat in the circle). He thinks about this but is clearly much less impressed by it than I am. So I try to impress him by adding that the theater is a place where you mustn't fly but must look at other people. He says he remembers reading about a play in Italy in which the actors came onstage and looked at the audience "instead." I say, "So you might be wondering in the theater, How can I get them to look at me?" He mumbles agreement and then says, slightly mocking me, I think, with one of my own words, "You mean the actors are rivals." I say, "Actors seem like people who are permitted to do forbidden things, to play other parts." And he says with some quickness in his voice, "I've always been waiting for someone to ask me to do something I'm not allowed, but once they've invited me then it's allowed!" After this new description of the trap there is a pause in which it seems as though we are both mulling the last bit over. I'm thinking, among a lot of other things, that he has told me what he has come to analysis for; and that even if someone is an oculist it doesn't mean that he necessarily has good eyesight, good enough to be able to fly. He then says that he feels something has really happened in this session—and certainly his words no longer feel like spectators—but he adds that he knows that when he goes to the theater next he will feel that he is going to die of anxiety; and I find myself thinking, Why not agree to die and see what happens?

The childhood memory that helped us push off into the conversation is clearly very suggestive in terms of the relationship between what you can see, what you can put together, and the parts you are allowed to play. If flying had represented possibility for the eight-year-old boy, and possibility, at least from an oedipal perspective, was inspired by the forbidden, then the theater—or, indeed, any confined space—was the place to be. Flying would turn into falling, looking would become being seen, performance would turn into failure. The theater was the place where he was connected, through terror, with his wish to enact forbidden versions of himself. And forbidden versions, in this context, means both those disapproved of by the parents and those outside the parents' orbit of recognition. As a child one may experience as forbidden simply the versions of oneself that turned up under the blank stare of one's parents' blind spots. The child's most puzzling and urgent projects—which

can pursue him through life like Frankenstein's monster—
sometimes come to life in this no-man's-land. One of this man's
pictures of himself as an adolescent was of someone auditioning
in a completely empty theater.

Describing the way he made sketches, Bonnard wrote in
his notebook: "The practice of cropping of the visual field
almost always gives something which doesn't seem true. Composition at the second degree consists of *bringing back certain
elements which lie outside the rectangle.*"[9] The phobic person is
suspended between the first and the second degree of composition; he assumes, quite sensibly, that making the transition
will break the frame rather than, as Bonnard intimates, making
it a frame for something that seems true. He hovers in his
terror, unable to make that decisive transition.

If horror, as William James wrote, is a "vertiginous baffling
of the expectation," then phobic horror is a baffling of the
awareness of expectation; there is nothing but paralysis or flight.
But in thinking about phobias it's worth taking seriously the
difference between a phobic situation and a phobic object like
an insect. A phobic situation, broadly speaking, one can choose
to avoid, but a phobic object can turn up unexpectedly. One
might say, for example, that a person who imagines that his
hate could turn up at any moment, like an unwanted guest—
who has to live in a state of continual internal vigilance to
ensure that he will always be fair—might choose an object
rather than a situation. A situation phobia is a controlled temptation. And clearly the availability of, the potential for access
to, the phobic object or situation is an essential factor, because
it signifies access—and a person's attitude to this proximity—to
otherwise repressed states of mind or versions of oneself.

A sixteen-year-old girl was referred to me for provocative
behavior in school. She would do absurd things to enrage her
teachers like sitting in lessons with a shoe on her head, but as
though this was quite normal. She was popular with her peers,
who seemed to view her with a rather wary admiration. As we
talked about this for several weeks—linking it to the life she
led in her family—I began to suggest to her in bits and pieces

that being provocative was one of her ways of getting to know people; that in order to find out whether she could like people she had to find the hate in them. She was playing, as it were, hunt the monster to discover what the worst version of the other person was that she was going to have to comply with. As I repeated this in different ways I noticed that occasionally she became curious; and at the point at which her curiosity was aroused she would say, quite rightly, that none of this was helping. After one rather tedious version of this interpretation she mentioned that she was terrified of spiders; indeed, she often had nightmares about them. I asked her if she hated me when I bored her, and she grinned.

It began to occur to me that she could manage a self that hated only if it was incarnated in someone else. By being provocative it was as though she was continually expelling this version of herself, but also keeping it alive and close at hand (she told me that even though spiders terrified her she never killed them; partly, I think, because she needed to know that her hate was alive and well, and also that to kill one might confirm the murderous power of her hatred). Her references to spiders were sporadic, and when I referred to them she told me categorically that this was something she was not prepared to talk about. I said that sometimes I might need to but that I would always warn her so she could put her fingers in her ears. She would then be able to regulate what she heard.

It was after establishing this ritual that I noticed that she was becoming interested in her dreams; not, I should add, in my attempted interpretations, but in the dream scenes themselves. As she said, "You go to bed and you never know what you're going to see." After what seemed like months of endlessly reported dreams she arrived one day for a session to tell me that she had had "the spider dream" again, and it was clear she wanted something from me. I asked her if anything had happened recently that she had given in to and regretted having done so. Her first reaction was to say that she was always giving in to things; and it had been evident from talking to her that she was very much a parental child whose parents were always effectively saying to her, "You mustn't get cross, because we need your help." But then she added—as though this was an odd bit of the answer—that in school the previous day the teacher had asked the class a question and she had answered it. I wondered if secretly she had bitterly resented this, as though answering the question felt like playing his game. She replied that she had bitten her tongue at lunch. I said that I thought the dream might be a protest and that in order to get really furious she had to find a spider to let her do it. She said, "You mean if I was a spider I could be really horrible." I said, "Yes, spiders are good to hate people with"; there was a pause and then she said, "Say some more." I said that I thought that probably every week she gave in to lots of things almost without noticing, and that if she came across a spider she was suddenly reminded of how cross she was and how much those feelings frightened her. Sometimes, when she felt really insulted, as she had yesterday with the teacher, she needed a spider so much that she had to dream one up. She listened to this intently and then said, "So a spider's a bit like turning on a tap?" and I agreed.

> Ignorance of myself is something I must work at; it is something studied like a dead language.
>
> Stanley Cavell, *The Claim of Reason*

A useful way to think about a symptom is to ask how you could teach someone to have it (what would I need to do, or who would I have to appear to be, to persuade someone that open spaces are terrifying?). For the phobic person the object or the situation that inspires the terror is beyond skepticism; he will behave as though he knows exactly what it is, however absurd this may seem to himself or other people. All his skepticism is kept for the interpreters. In a phobia a person explicitly pretends to a private language, to a secretive exemption from shared meanings. The phobia reveals virtually nothing about the object except its supposed power to frighten; it baffles inquiry. Just as, in actuality, there is no repetition, only a wish for the idea of repetition as a way of familiarizing the present, so, with the phobic object or situation, the person thinks that he knows where he is. Better the devil you know than an angel you don't.

But it is, paradoxically, the very certainty of the phobic person that robs him of his autonomy (of course Freud would say that being a person robs him of his autonomy). Before the phobic object he submits to something akin to possession, to an experience without the mobility of perspectives. A phobia, like virtually nothing else, shows the capacity of the body to be gripped by occult meaning; it is like a state of somatic conviction. "The phobic object," Julia Kristeva writes in *Powers of Horror,* "is precisely avoidance of choice, it tries as long as possible to maintain the subject far from decision";[10] or from the notion that this could be a matter for decision. It is as though the object is issuing the orders, and the body responds even in anticipation of its presence. As the victim of terror the subject is as far as possible, in his own mind, from being the one who terrorizes. But he is sustaining a relationship, even in his avoidance, constituted by terror. "Such avoidances," the psychoanalyst Roger Money-Kyrle remarked, "are superimposed upon seekings."[11]

If a phobia has the effect of empowering and disempowering a person at the same time—like a kind of quotidian sublime, filling him with terror and rendering him helpless—it is also, by the same token, a way of making ordinary places and things extremely charged, like an unconscious estrangement technique. To be petrified by a pigeon is a way of making it new. The phobia is eroticization not so much of danger as of significance. The creation toward the end of the nineteenth century of these new sexual objects—the familiar phobias became "symptoms" in the 1870s—the discovery that a panic akin to sexual excitement was felt by certain people when confronted with birds, rodents, insects, theaters, or open spaces, could be used as evidence of the idea of an unconscious mind; or of irrational selves inhabiting respectable selves, as in Jekyll and Hyde (Stevenson's tale was published in 1886). But those who made category mistakes—pigeons, after all, are not killers—had to be categorized. The advantage of pathologizing—and, of course, self-pathologizing—is that it appears to place the participants in a structure of preexisting knowledge and authority.

The very absurdity of phobias, often even to the people who have them, could seem like a parody of the diagnostic process.

As symptoms, phobias provide a useful focus for what Donald Davidson has described as "the underlying paradox of irrationality"; "if we explain it too well," he writes, "we turn it into a concealed form of rationality; while if we assign incoherence too glibly, we merely compromise our ability to diagnose irrationality by withdrawing the background of rationality needed to justify any diagnosis at all."[12] One of the functions of a phobia is to fix such distinctions, to take the paradox out of them (phobia, ritualized as taboo, maintains a sensible universe). For the phobic person the phobia guarantees the difference—marks out a boundary—between the acceptably safe and the dangerously forbidden and exciting; and for his double, the interpreter, between the rational and the irrational (so one could ask, for example, "What would I have to say about one of my dislikes to make you think I was phobic of it, rather than just very discriminating?" or "Are we phobic of all the things we never do and all the places we never go, unconsciously phobic, as it were?"). The catastrophe that the phobic and his interpreter are both trying to avert is the collapse of their distinctions, the loss, or rather the mixing, of their categories. Practicing the martial arts of purity and danger, what can they do for each other beyond providing mutual reassurance?

Symptoms are a way of thinking about difficult things, thinking with the sound turned off, as it were. One of the reasons, perhaps, that Freud was so intrigued by phobias—several of the great case histories are analyses of phobias—was that the making of a phobia was the model for the making of a theory. A phobia, like a psychoanalytic theory, is a story about where the wild things are. And these theories, like their phobic paradigm, organize themselves around a fantasy of the impossible, the unacceptable in its most extreme form. Because Freud refused to assign incoherence too glibly—realizing that the rational and the irrational have to double for each other—he began to describe curiosity and knowledge, including, of course, the knowledge that is psychoanalytic theory, as reactive

to fear; an attempt to master the phobia—the first recognition—
that by inaugurating consciousness depletes it. If terror is the
object of knowledge, knowledge is counterphobic.

In order to become what Freud thinks of as a person, one
has to become phobic; and one can become phobic only by
believing that there are an external and an internal world that
are discrete. "What is bad, what is alien to the ego and what is
external are, to begin with, identical," Freud writes in "Negation," his extraordinary paper of 1925. For the ego to sustain
itself as good, which means in Freud's terms for the ego to
sustain itself, depends upon expelling everything experienced
as bad into the outside world. The assumption is that at the
very beginning unpleasure is soon intolerable and spells death
and that consciousness is of unpleasure. The "bad"—or Melanie
Klein would say the hate—is, pre-oedipally, the excess of desire
that threatens to destroy the ego and, slightly later, the object;
and oedipally, the forbidden incestuous desires. "In so far as the
objects which are presented to it are sources of pleasure," Freud
writes in "Instincts and Their Vicissitudes" (1915), "the ego
takes them into itself, 'introjects' them . . . and, on the other
hand, it expels whatever within itself becomes a cause of unpleasure." [13] The first world we find outside is, in part, a repository
for the terror inside us, an elsewhere for those desires and
objects that bring unpleasure. And that world we make outside
is the world we need to get away from. It is the place, or one
of the places, where we put the objects and desires we wish did
not belong to us. To be at home in the world we need to keep
it inhospitable.

The ego needs a place elsewhere—which will be called
outside—and another place elsewhere that Freud will call "the
repressed unconscious," which is inside. And this matches, of
course, the good/bad distinction (a different way of putting it
might be to say: there's no such thing as an internal world—or
an external world; there are just collections of words that seem
to do justice to the complexity of what we feel). But in Freud's
terms the ego, in this process of distributing the bad things, is
depleting itself in the hopeless task of keeping itself what Freud

calls a "pure pleasure ego." The developmental question, in Freud's view—conceived of, or rather enacted, before the individual could describe it like this—is, what is unbearable about oneself and where is one going to put it? And the consequent preoccupation becomes, once one has supposedly got rid of it, how is one going to live in a state of such impoverishment, so emptied of oneself? The phobic object becomes the promise— the (unconscious) gift returned, as it were—that has to be refused. But the refusal, of course, is a way of keeping the promise.

If, as Freud believed, one is fundamentally unable—or ill-equipped in childhood—to contain oneself, then it is part of the developmental project to find a phobia, to localize the impossible in oneself elsewhere. But of course for Freud fantasies—and the fantasy that makes a phobia—are forms of magical thinking; in the phobic fantasy you convince a part of yourself that the bad things are elsewhere only because there is really no elsewhere (or the only real elsewhere is the place you cannot put parts of yourself). Finding hate-objects may be every bit as essential as finding love-objects, but if one can tolerate some of one's badness—meaning recognize it as yours—then one can take some fear out of the world. In this psychoanalytic picture the treatment is a method of retrieval; almost, one might say, of the misplaced persons in oneself. With this picture, though, psychoanalysis can become unwittingly punitive, because each person has a limit to what he can take (not to mention the fact that there is a tyrannically omniscient fantasy at work here of what constitutes a "whole" person). In Freud's view, the ego depends upon its phobia. It is, so to speak, its first relationship, and one that is inevitably paranoid (paranoia being, as it were, a refusal to be left out).

The idea of the unconscious is, among other things, a way of describing the fact that there are things we didn't know we could say. A phobia is a conviction that bad things are unspeakable, and therefore that the unspeakable is always bad. And this makes tacit understandings for the phobic person always dangerous. If you articulate the terror for the phobic person he may be persecuted by it again, and if you don't you collude with the notion that there is something truly unbearable.

Phobias, that is to say, confront the psychoanalyst very starkly, with the dilemma of cure. The art of psychoanalysis, for both the participants, is to produce interesting redescriptions: redescriptions that the patient is free—can bear—to be interested in. Or to put it another way: the aim of psychoanalysis is not to cure people but to show them that there is nothing wrong with them.

- 3 -

On Risk and Solitude

What sort of space is that which separates a man from
his fellows and makes him solitary? I have found that no
exertion of the legs can bring two minds much nearer
to one another. What do we want most to dwell near to?

Henry David Thoreau, *Walden*

An affinity for solitude is comparable only to one's affinity for
certain other people. And yet one's first experience of solitude,
like one's first experience of the other, is fraught with danger.
"In children," Freud writes, "the first phobias relating to situations are those of darkness and solitude. The former of these
often persists throughout life; both are involved when a child
feels the absence of some loved person who looks after it—
its mother, that is to say."[1] The absence of the visible and
the absence of an object; and the risk, as in dreams, that inner-
most thoughts will come to light. For this reason, perhaps,
it is the phobia relating to solitude that for some people persists throughout life. Freud's preference here, toward darkness
but away from solitude, reflects the fact that in his work, as
opposed to his life, there is, as it were, a repression of solitude,
of its theoretical elaboration. Although narcissism, the dream,
mourning, the death work all testify to Freud's conception of
the human subject as profoundly solitary, the index of the
Standard Edition, for example, contains only two references to
solitude. It is as though solitude itself, like the holding environment of early infancy, is taken for granted by Freud. It is
perhaps the only risk of childhood whose counterpart in adult
life he fails explicitly to consider.

Discussing other "situation phobias" in the *Introductory Lectures,* Freud uses examples of various kinds of journey:

We know that there is more chance of an accident when we are on a railway journey than when we stay at home— the chance of a collision; we know, too, that a ship may go down, in which case there is a possibility of being drowned; but we don't think of these dangers, and travel by rail and ship without anxiety. It cannot be disputed that we should fall into the river if the bridge collapsed at the moment we were crossing it; but that happens so exceedingly seldom that it does not arise as a danger. Solitude, too, has its dangers and in certain circumstances we avoid it; but there is no question of our not being able to tolerate it under any conditions even for a moment.[2]

Solitude does not occur to us, perhaps, as being like a journey, and journeys of the kind Freud mentions are usually spent in the presence of other people. Freud is overinsistent that we can tolerate solitude but silent about its dangers. From the logic of his examples we could infer, but only in the most speculative way, that the dangers of solitude were linked in his mind with being dropped (the idea, in D. W. Winnicott's sense, of being dropped as an infant). Freud, as we know, was made anxious by traveling; and in the *Introductory Lectures* themselves he associates journeys with death. "Dying," he writes, in the Section "Symbolism in Dreams," "is replaced in dreams by departure, by a train journey." Travelers, whether they acknowledge it or not, are traveling toward death. "The dramatist is using the same symbolic connection," he writes, "when he speaks of the after-life as 'the undiscovered country from whose bourne no *traveller* returns.'"[3] The dream, after all, is the soliloquy of the unconscious, and it is clearly not gratuitous that Freud, to elucidate an element in the dream, uses here that most famous witnessed solitude of Hamlet's soliloquy.

It is the infant waiting too long for his mother that is traveling toward death because, unattended, he is in the solitary confinement of his body. Solitude is a journey, a potentially fatal journey, for an infant in the absence of sufficient maternal care. But it is worth remembering that the infant in the dark, the infant by himself, is not only waiting for the mother. Sleep, for example, is not exclusively a state of anticipation. It is, of course, difficult to conceive in psychoanalytic terms of an absence that is not, in some way, anticipatory.

Through desire the child discovers his solitude, and through solitude his desire. He depends upon a reliable but ultimately elusive object that can appease but never finally satisfy him. But from the very beginning, quite unwittingly, he has involved an object. "The subject," Jacques Lacan writes, "has never done anything other than demand, he could not have survived otherwise; and we just follow on from there."[4] We follow on in a curious solitude *à deux* called the analytic situation. And in that setting we find, again and again, that the patient is faced with the risk of entrusting himself. Indeed, one of the aims of the analysis will be to reveal the full nature of the risk. In the induced regression of analytic treatment the patient is invited—to redescribe the "golden rule"—to hand over to the analyst something that we refer to, after Winnicott, as a holding function. In free association the patient takes the risk of not knowing what he is going to say. The patient's most difficult task will be fully to allow himself his symptomatology.

The clamorously dependent infant with a sufficiently attentive mother ends up, so the normative story goes, as an adult with a capacity for solitude, for whom withdrawal is an escape not merely, or solely, from persecution, but toward a replenishing privacy. But dependence, we assume, does not simply disappear; somewhere, we think, there is an object, or the shadow of an object. So, in states of solitude what does the adult depend upon? To what does he risk entrusting himself?

The risks involved in traveling that Freud described could be tolerated, he suggested, because they were, in actual terms, minimal. But in the case of more serious kinds of risk—those which are not exclusively counterphobic—of which solitude can be one, the individual is attempting to find, often unconsciously, that which is beyond his omnipotent control but not, by virtue of being so, persecutory. (A good example of this is Francis Bacon describing the point at which he needs to throw paint at his pictures as part of the process of composition.) I am referring here not to compulsive risk-taking, which is always constituted by a fantasy of what has already been lost—only the impossible, as we know, is addictive—but to the ordinary risks of adolescence that extend into adult life. A sixteen-year-old boy, for example, in his own words a "loner" and a "risk merchant," tells me in a session about the moment, at age ten, when he eventually learned to swim after having been terrified of water: "I knew I was safer out of my depth because even though I couldn't stand, there was more water to hold me up." One of the central paradoxes for the adolescent is his discovery that only the object beyond his control can be found to be reliable. For the boy the risk of learning to swim was the risk of discovering that he, or rather his body, would float. The heart of swimming is that you can float. Standing within his depth, apparently in control, was the omnipotence born of anxiety; the opposite of omnipotence here was not impotence, as he had feared, but his being able to entrust himself to the water. The defense of vigilant self-holding precluded his being able to swim. He needed "a generous kind of negligence" with himself.[5] It is possible to be too concerned about oneself.

This developmental process can be usefully understood in terms of epistemology, although of course it could hardly be experienced in these terms. Iris Murdoch, in her book on Sartre, compares him to his detriment with Adorno, whom she describes as picturing "'knowledge as an attentive, truthful, patience with the contingent, where the latter is not a hostile Other to be overcome, but more like an ordinary world-round-about-us.' Approaching knowledge of the object is the act in which the subject rends the veil it is weaving around the object. It can do this only where, fearlessly passive, it entrusts itself to its own experience."[6] In developmental terms the "hostile Other" can represent the failure of the holding environment. My patient could swim once the water was like an ordinary world-round-about-him, when he could be "fearlessly passive" out of his depth. And the adolescent, we might add along similar lines, in his florid resumption of sexuality is both weaving and rending a veil around the new object, his pubescent body.

The infant depends on the mother and her care to prevent him from being out of his depth; in adolescence, as we know, this protection is both wished for and defied. Risks are taken as part of the mastery of noncompliance. One way the adolescent differentiates himself, discovers his capacity for solitude—for a self-reliance that is not merely a triumph over his need for the object—is by taking and making risks. He needs, unconsciously, to endanger his body, to experiment with the representations of it, and he does this out of the most primitive form of solitude, isolation. As Winnicott has written,

> The adolescent is essentially an isolate. It is from a position of isolation that he or she launches out into what may result in relationships . . . The adolescent is repeating an essential phase of infancy, for the infant too is an isolate, at least until he or she has been able to establish the capacity for relating to objects that are outside magical control. The infant becomes able to recognise and to welcome the existence of objects that are not part of the infant, but this is an achievement. The adolescent repeats this struggle.[7]

The adolescent's body—and it is part of the adolescent project to inhabit and be inhabited by the body—can be experienced in its newfound sexuality as an object, and an object that is manifestly outside magical control. For the adolescent, Winnicott writes, "relationships must first be tried out on subjective objects."[8] He does not mention the sense in which the body—and this sense comes to consciousness at puberty—is by definition both a subjective object and an object objectively perceived. To the adolescent it is, like the analyst in the transference, the most familiar stranger. In puberty the adolescent develops what can be accurately referred to as a transference to his own body; what crystallize in adolescence, what return partly as enactment through risk, are doubts about the mother and the holding environment of infancy. These doubts are transferred on to the body, turned against it, as it begins to represent a new kind of internal environment, a more solitary one. That is to say, the adolescent begins to realize that the original mother is his body.

It is not that the adolescent is attempting to "own his body"—that absurd commodity of ego-psychology—as part of his separation from the mother, nor is he simply taking over her caregiving aspects. He is testing the representations of the body acquired through early experience. Is it a safe house? Is it reliable? Does it have other allegiances? What does it promise, and why does it refuse? These are the questions, and one can imagine others, that the infant, if he could, might ask of the mother, and that the adolescent re-presents as mood and enactment. In the usual risks of adolescence—that stage of legitimate criminality and illicit solitude—the adolescent survives danger in a kind of virtual or "as if" absence of maternal care. And this, of course, has implications for treatment, since in the psychoanalytic literature an interest in risk-taking has usually been related to pathology; as integral, for example, to the perversions. (We may wonder, conversely, what the absence of risk signifies in a person's life.) It may be, for example, that some perversions are an albeit sexualized way of keeping alive a risk-taking part of the self. When the adolescent, like the adult, is alone, he is alone in the presence of his own body, and his own body becomes at this stage an acute preoccupation. What kind of maternal and/or paternal object, or what other kind of object, does his body represents to him, and how does he find out? In the taking and making of bodily risks he begins to constitute his own possibility for a benign solitude, reliably alone in the presence of the body and its thoughts. The world and his body can feel as dangerous to the adolescent, and not only to the adolescent, as the risks he has failed to take with them. His capacity for a beneficent solitude will depend on his being able to entrust himself to his body as a sufficiently holding environment. And he will transfer on to his own body, recreate inside it, as it were, the holding environment of infancy in considerable detail.

A point comes in the treatment, Freud once said, when the patient must be encouraged to do the thing he most fears. It is this that the adolescent knows and refuses to know, and that his analyst finds more than a little difficult to deal with.

I paid the price of solitude
But at least I'm out of debt.

    Bob Dylan, "Dirge"

Adolescence, as we know, recapitulates something of infancy
but in dramatically modified form. From adolescence onward
the link between risk and solitude becomes a vivid and traumatic
issue. But the pressing question of risk is clearly bound up with
something that certain psychoanalysts after Freud have seen as
central to early development: a capacity for concern. We create
risk when we endanger something we value, whenever we test
the relationship between thrills and virtues. So to understand,
or make conscious, what constitutes a risk for us—our own
personal repertoire of risks—is an important clue about what it
is that we do value; and it also enjoins us to consider the pleasures of carelessness. It is a paradox of some interest that
although psychoanalysis was, from the very beginning, about
the relationship between justice and love, there is no explicit or
coercive description in Freud's work of what constitutes a good
life; and this is one of the many things that distinguishes him
from his critics and followers. It is, however, part of our traditional morality to assume—and this is reflected in Kleinian
theory—that concern for other people is integral to a good life.
It is therefore another interesting paradox in the development
of psychoanalysis to note how much, for Winnicott, development depended on the capacity to relinquish or suspend concern
for the object. Indeed, where else can we go in psychoanalytic
theory for descriptions of a benign disregard of objects that
extends into adult life? I am not saying that Winnicott, in his
writing, did not mention concern; indeed, one of the few
developmental stages he dared name was a Stage of Concern.
Nor am I saying that I think Winnicott was a proto-Nietz-
schean—although I do believe he has a truly frightening and
exhilarating theory of development. But I am saying that Winnicott's writing, by virtue of being writing, is, like Freud's,
riven with crosscurrents and packed with contradiction. And
one of the insistent themes in his writing, though it is usually

understated and always qualified, is that concern for an object is easily a compliant act and always potentially an obstacle to passionate intimacy and personal development. And this has interesting implications for the relationship that increasingly preoccupied Winnicott as he got older: the relationship one has with oneself. We could wonder, for example, what we are starving ourselves of by being too concerned about ourselves.

The first unwitting risk of infancy is the infant's being entrusted to the mother's care. Optimally the mother adapts collaboratively to the infant's needs, to create what Winnicott calls a state of illusion:

> the baby has instinctual urges and predatory ideas. The mother has a breast and the power to produce milk, and the idea that she would like to be attacked by a hungry baby. These two phenomena do not come into relation with each other till the mother and child live an experience together. I think of the process as if two lines came from opposite directions, liable to come near each other. If they overlap there is a moment of illusion—a bit of experience which the infant can take as either his hallucination or a thing belonging to external reality.[9]

It is a moment of illusion because, in a good feed, from the infant's point of view, he has created out of desire what he has, in fact, found. The mother, for the infant, is of course not what we would think of as a real person. As Stephen Mitchell puts it, "the infant is almost oblivious to the mother as a person; she 'brings the world' to the infant and is the invisible agent of his needs."[10] If she insists on being a real person, then the infant or young child has to invent a false self to deal with her. What Winnicott calls the False Self is invented to manage a prematurely important object. The False Self enacts a kind of dissociated regard or recognition of the object; the object is taken seriously, is shown concern, but not by a person. Pathology, in Winnicott's terms, is the result of the object's demand—or assumed demand—for concern. At the very beginning, from Winnicott's point of view, concern is always spurious. So how does the infant get to feel "genuine concern," whatever that might mean?

Winnicott posits a "primitive ruthlessness" to characterize the infant's desire; this ruthlessness for Winnicott is not sadism—does not include a sexual pleasure in hurting—but is simply the way the infant, if he is enabled, carelessly loves the mother. But this story of the fluent passionate life quite soon complicates into disillusionment. The infant, "naturally," in Winnicott's view, begins slowly to register the mother as separate and begins to feel guilty. Thus, introducing his 1957 paper "Psychoanalysis and the Sense of Guilt," he says that he will "attempt to study guilt feeling not as a thing to be inculcated but as an aspect of the development of the individual . . . Those who hold the view that morality needs to be inculcated teach small children accordingly, and they forgo the pleasure of watching morality develop naturally in their children, who are thriving in a good setting that is provided in a personal and individual way." [11]

In this apparently rather reassuring account the child's innate morality, his own moral values, develop; unforced, the child's original goodness, the rudimentary virtues of cooperation and imaginative empathy, simply turn up. It is worth noting, though, that in Winnicott's view development does not happen in the service of morality; rather, morality happens in the service of development. The child's own moral values, like his symptomatology, work for him only insofar as they protect his growth. That is to say, personal development necessitates a certain moral opportunism. "Those who lack moral sense"— which is different from a moral sense—"have lacked at the early stages of their development the emotional and physical setting which would have enabled the capacity for guilt sense to have developed." "Gradually," he writes, "a capacity for guilt sense builds up in the individual in relation to the mother, and this is intimately related to the opportunity for reparation." Winnicott offers a simple sequence, derived, he says, from Klein's work, in which his own distinctive additions are characteristically understated. From Klein, he claims in a rather disingenuous piece of redescription, he had understood that "the primitive love impulse has an aggressive aim; being ruthless it carries with it a variable quantity of destructive ideas unaffected by concern." He describes the innumerable repetitions spread over a period of time, which he calls the "benign circle"—the opposite, one assumes, of a vicious circle—and which constitutes Klein's depressive position.[12] It's worth noting that a circle takes you back to where you started from. Reparation could be merely the unwillingness to tolerate the unknown consequences of one's actions, a preemptive strike against the future.

The benign circle, which Winnicott will eventually redescribe in the most unexpected way, follows this pattern. First, there is the instinctual experience of a wholehearted feed; second, acceptance of responsibility by the infant for the fantasized ravages of his desire, which is referred to as guilt; third, there is the working through of this regret and fear, which takes the infant to the fourth stage of the "true restitutive gesture." This benign circle relies upon the mother, in a way that Klein herself never emphasized. It depends absolutely, according to Winnicott, "on the mother's capacity to survive the instinctual moment, and so to be there to receive and understand the true reparative gesture." It is assumed that there is regret built into desire, because it is imagined by the infant as an act of robbery and damage; and so it is crucial that the mother can respond to the child's wish, in that telling phrase, to make up. Only if the mother accepts reparation is the infant able, according to Winnicott, "to accept responsibility for the total fantasy of the full instinctual impulse that was previously ruthless. Ruthlessness gives way to ruth, unconcern to concern."[13]

But Winnicott then refers, in a brief paragraph that contradicts the rest of his paper, to a figure he calls the "creative artist," who, in a way he doesn't explain, is apparently exempt from the benign circle he has described, who has in fact dispensed with this circle altogether. For this person reparation, and the gratitude and sense of indebtedness it implies, is irrelevant, simply the creation of an obstacle. Characterized by his ruthlessness, the artist's particular kind of socialization "obviates the need for guilt feeling and the associated reparative and restitutive activity that forms the basis of ordinary constructive work." *Obviate* is an interesting word here, meaning as it does "to meet on the way, to prevent or dispose of in advance, to forestall."[14] The artist's life then, which "obviates the need for guilt feeling," is one in which he has noticed guilt but has found ways of preempting it. He has refused to feel guilty, or rather, to feel hampered by it. Winnicott concludes his eleven-and-a-half-line section "The Creative Artist" in an appropriately tantalizing way: "Ordinary guilt-ridden people find this bewildering yet they have a sneaking regard for ruthlessness that does in fact, in such circumstances, achieve more than guilt-driven labour."[15] In terms of the rhetoric of his statement, I think it is fair to say that most of us would rather think of ourselves as creative artists than as endlessly involved in what Winnicott calls, in an implicit critique of Klein's entire work, "guilt-driven labour" (wherever suffering is moralized, as it is in Klein's Depressive Position, it is always idealized). If the psychoanalyst, for example, was this kind of creative artist, rather than compulsively reparative, what would his work be like?

In this quite sudden and surprising interruption of his text Winnicott is suggesting an alternative to the depressive position. Having already redescribed Klein's apparently fundamental concept in which the infant begins to recognize that the object that he destroys in fantasy is the object that he loves, that he suffers an intense and formative anguish over this that can be allayed only by his reparative gestures, Winnicott then presents us with what we must call, for the sake of discussion, the creative artist, who, Winnicott says, "may in fact fail to understand, or even may despise the feelings of concern that motivate a less creative person."[16] What are we to make of this? We know that Winnicott shares the post-Romantic idealization of the artist as exemplary man; as the most real person, authentic by virtue of his noncompliance. But Winnicott is using the figure of the artist here to allow himself, in a psychoanalytic setting, his own original and disturbing version of development. Interestingly, this paper was delivered as one of six public lectures at the Institute of Psycho-Analysis in London to celebrate the centenary of Freud's birth the same year that Klein's seminal essay

"Envy and Gratitude" was published. The paper signifies the deferred birth of Winnicott's distinctive developmental theory.

The first risk of development, recreated in the analytic setting, involves the infant and child's entrusting himself to the mother's holding environment. But the object, the mother, becomes real—changes, in Winnicott's language, from a subjective object to an object more objectively perceived—only through being destroyed in fantasy and yet being seen to survive the hatred. It is, as it were, people's resilience that makes them real for us. "It is the destruction of the object that places the object outside of the area of the subject's omnipotent control. In these ways the object develops its own autonomy and life and, if it survives, contributes in to the subject, according to its own properties."[17]

If the object can survive the full blast of the subject's hatred, then the person can conceive of the object as beyond his power and therefore as fully real; that is to say, not reconstituted by the subject's reparation but constituted by its own survival. But this process as Winnicott describes it involves a curious paradox: only by suspending concern for the object is the object established as real; only by not caring for the object—hating it wholeheartedly—can we get to know it (as a subject). By diminishing one's regard for the object—ceasing to overprotect the object from oneself—real contact is made. Two solitudes are established. But the claiming of one's solitude, which is inextricable from this battle, is a ruthless act. Winnicott sees development as involving increasingly sophisticated forms of disregard for the object, but to make possible real contact with a real object. So the second developmental risk, in this overly schematic account, entails relinguishing concern for the object. Only through our development of the capacity to treat people as objects can they become real for us. And this provides us with another way of looking at perversions, a subject about which, significantly, Winnicott has little explicitly to say. It is as though, in perverse sadomasochistic contracts, the process Winnicott describes is short-circuited. Hatred of and disregard for the object are aided and abetted by the object's collusive agreement. That is to say, the object does not survive—robustly refuse to be dominated—but capitulates, agrees to be destroyed or damaged. So what is described in the psychoanalytic literature as a perverse contract—the master and slave configuration of sadomasochism—is a self-thwarting attempt to undo a symbiotic bond. An obstacle is created by the sadomasochistic couple at the point at which they might, in Winnicott's language, move over from being subjective objects for each other to being real, beyond each other's omnipotent control. It is the solitude of being separate that they cannot risk. There is also, one should remember, a terror of the absence of dependence.

Development itself, which Winnicott in his later work regarded as an intrinsically creative process, was bound up for him with a capacity for ruthlessness. There was the primary ruthless desire of infancy—an elemental state of mind—that had, to some degree, to be carried forward into adult life. And creativity—what Winnicott later called creative living—involved the search for, and attempt to establish, a medium, an environment, a relationship that could survive the person's most passionate destructiveness. The risk in destructiveness is that it may not be withstood; the risk of establishing one's solitude is the risk of one's potential freedom.

Clearly, the need to make reparation binds one to objects. So where does Winnicott's enigmatic creative artist fit into this, who has dispensed with reparation and who, in Winnicott's own words, "may despise feelings of concern that motivate a less creative person"? We cannot ignore the equation here of concern with diminished creativity. "Of the artist," Winnicott writes in his curious celebration, "it may be said that some have no capacity for guilt."[18] And far from suggesting that there is anything wrong with such a person, Winnicott is quite clear that for him this figure of the artist, some of whose characteristics are usually associated in psychoanalysis with perversion, or even psychopathy, is a kind of ego-ideal. The figure Winnicott calls the creative artist is certainly determined not to be thwarted by concern for other people. Indeed, he or she may be thought of as somebody with a certain kind of primary relationship with himself. Perhaps the artist has the courage of his perversions?

> In my solitude
> I have seen things very clearly
> which are not true.

> Antonio Machado, *Twenty Proverbs*

Writing to Countess de Solm-Laubach on August 3, 1907, the poet Rilke expressed in extreme form what may be, or could be, a common experience: "except for two short interruptions, I have not pronounced a single word for weeks; at last my solitude has closed in and I am in my work like a pit in its fruit." The implication is that speaking—involvement with other people—would have held off this nurturing solitude in which his work could grow. He relinquishes an environment of external objects and becomes the seed of himself.

In states of absorption, in the solitude of concentration, the other object that disappears is the body. The good-enough environment of the body can be taken for granted; it is most reliably present by virtue of its absence. It does not, as it does in states of desire and illness, insist on its importance; in Maurice Blanchot's words, one "yields to the risk of the absence of time."[19] A fertile solitude is a benign forgetting of the body that takes care of itself; and in this context desire becomes a remembering. In the dream, Freud tells us—that most solitary representation—the body must not be disturbed; we must not wake up to it. A productive solitude, the solitude in which what could never have been anticipated appears, is linked with a quality of attention. The excessive proximity of the object, or of the body as intrusive object, is always a preemptive presence. "That is why I go into solitude," Nietzsche wrote, "so as not to drink out of everybody's cistern. When I am among the many I live as the many do, and I do not think as I really think; after a time it always seems as though they want to banish me from myself and rob me of my soul."[20] From the facilitating object to the object as usurping presence: somewhere here the analyst finds himself, placed in the patient's transference. But what of the journey from dependence to the wish for solitude, a wish that takes us beyond, or at least outside, the analytic situation? Although the wish for solitude can be a denial of dependence, a capacity for solitude may be its fullest acknowledgment.

For Winnicott the capacity to be alone depended upon the earlier experience of the child alone in the presence of the mother. He does not, of course, speak of the child alone in the presence of his father, nor in detail of what Masud Khan has called "the infant-in-care alone with himself."[21] The precursor of the capacity for solitude is the child in the reliable, unimpinging presence of the mother who would cover the risks. If the mother is there, he can lose himself in a game; and optimally, in Winnicott's work, mother is always there presiding over our solitude. But the human subject in Freud—a desiring solitude—lives between absence and conflict. Freud could not conceive, in his own psychoanalytic terms, of a solitude that was constituted as a full presence rather than as a lack; and psychoanalysis, of course, has an impoverished vocabulary for states of plenitude that are not considered pathological. For Freud solitude could be described only as an absence, for Winnicott only as a presence. It is a significant measure of difference.

And still the question remains: to what do we risk entrusting ourselves in solitude? Although God is no longer our perpetual witness, we have our own available ghosts, our constitutive psychoanalytic fictions—the unconscious, the good internal object, the developmental process, the body and its destiny, language. Perhaps in solitude we are, as we say, simply "on our own." Is it not, after all, the case that the patient comes to analysis to reconstitute his solitude through the other, the solitude that only he can know?

- 4 -

On Composure

I had fancied that the value of life lay in its inscrutable possibilities; in the fact that I never know, in addressing myself to a new individual, what may befall me.

Ralph Waldo Emerson, *Experience*

It's something we lose but tend not to find: we think of composure, like confidence, as something we regain. It is as though the composure has already happened, when actually composure is always, as one might say, after the fact, a paradoxical form of self-cure for the experience of traumatic excitement; or rather, the seduction of one's own excitement. Indeed, the notion of composure is a clue about the fantasies—all the unspoken words—we have about excitement. It is worth considering what we imagine we are composing, and whom we imagine this particular composition will satisfy.

When Adam expresses, in book 9 of *Paradise Lost,* what turn out to be shrewd uncertainties at Eve's suggestion that they should garden separately in Paradise, she replies "with sweet austere composure." A need to compose at that critical moment, something at once palatable and worthy of considered respect. But the composure is itself ominous, a sign of elaborate calculation, an implicit acknowledgment that there are now parts of Eve that need to be composed. "To compose," as Ruskin wrote, "is to arrange unequal things."

Composure, if it is a quality, is the least innocent of the virtues; *Roget's Thesaurus,* for example, offers "inexcitability" as a synonym. Provoked by an excess of excitement, composure becomes a way of accommodating such experience, a belated refusal; it becomes, in fact, a superstition of confidence in the integrity of the self. It is of interest, then, that composure has never become part of the language of psychoanalysis, divided

as it has always been over issues of self-possession—the problem and the pleasure of pleasure. One could, for example, redescribe some of the familiar psychoanalytic categories in terms
of the subject's conscious and unconscious attitudes to his or
her composure: the "pervert" flirts with his composure; the
"hysteric" simulates its absence; the "obsessional" parodies it;
and so on. The idea of composure can be seen as integral to
Freud's fiction of the ego. Just as the ego is the "seat of anxiety,"
so, by the same token, it is the seat of composure. The ego
composes the body in fantasy. So those most furtively absorbing and exciting ideas, masturbation fantasies, can be seen as
stories or scenarios in which, through careful disguise, one
makes it safe to have an excited body; or rather, the spectacle
of an excited body. Desire is always staged, as it were, by the
ego.

For Freud stimulation was impingement, instinctual life
sustaining the organism and yet throwing it into disarray. As
he wrote in *Beyond the Pleasure Principle,* with characteristic misgiving, "Protection against stimuli is an almost more important
function for the living organism than reception of stimuli";[1] as
though what is to be received is always potentially in excess.
Jean Laplanche has extended Freud's sense of the individual's
radical besiegement with his concept of "the attack of the drives
on the ego."[2] The ego is appointed, in the Freudian story, somehow to diminish the trauma of the body, but the body has no
time for the ego's rage for order. Composure becomes a preemptive strike—a kind of machine inside the ghost—against
this fundamental disarray.

In the course of development, and apparently to differing
degrees, the body has to lose its overwhelming immediacy for
the child, to become the child's most paradoxical belonging.
Composure would begin as the way the child responds, at least
initially, to the intimated demand by the mother, in the face of
the child's desire for her, that the child alter the form of its self-
presentation. An original clamorousness becomes a calculated
social poise, a distinctive awkwardness that bears witness to the
child's struggle for acceptable forms of excitement, for ways in
which he can be seen to be a desiring subject without losing face.

In Freudian terms composure would be a form, largely unconscious, of vigilant self-control. But with his flair for the ingenuous—a characteristic disregard for the special language of psychoanalysis—Winnicott gives us a different way of considering the idea of composure. Where Freud sees the possibility for mastery, Winnicott sees the possibility for surprise. Where Freud is preoccupied with defensive forms of control, Winnicott emphasizes something less virile, which he calls "holding." Holding describes the early maternal care that makes possible the infant's psychosomatic integration; and holding implies reciprocal accommodations, exactly what one observes in the subtle process of someone's carrying or picking up a child. In Winnicott's terms, composure can be seen as a deferral, a kind of self-holding that keeps open the possibility of finding an environment in which the composure itself could be relinquished. Composure would, by definition, seek its own negation. It might, in other words, be part of a person's developmental project to create or find an environment in which his composure was of no use, and in which this fact was no longer a problem (sadomasochism, one could say, is the endlessly orchestrated disappointment of this wish).

In a remarkable early paper Winnicott implicitly addresses the question, What use does one want to make of the idea of mind?—an idea conspicuous by its absence in British writing on Freud. In "The Mind and Its Relation to the Psyche-Soma" (1949), Winnicott suggests, neglecting Freud's metapsychology, that the individual uses what he calls "mental functioning" in order to make up for failures of mothering. One mothers oneself, or rather, foster-mothers one's self, with one's mind. Ordinarily the mind is "no more than a special case of the functioning of the psyche-soma . . . the imaginative elaboration of somatic parts, feelings and functions, that is, of physical aliveness."[3] It is an expression of the body-self through fantasy. As he writes elsewhere, in normal development "the infant's mind [is] able to account for and so to allow for failures of adaptation. In this way the mind is allied to the mother and takes over part of her function." Bad mind, or what Winnicott would call the precocious mind, quickens in reaction to excessive maternal unpredictability. "As a more common result of the lesser degrees of tantalizing infant care in the earliest stages we find mental functioning becoming a thing in itself, practically replacing the good mother and making her unnecessary."[4] The tantalized child turns away from the mother in a bewilderment that he will organize into a diffuse resentment. Engendered by a grudge, the precocious mind of the child stops him from depending, or rather, enables him to simulate independence. For the child, like the adult, there is always the anonymous company of thoughts. And there is always the mind as the theater of revenge. In fact Winnicott seems to imply that the figure he calls "the intellectual" is always retaliating, always backing a grudge.

There is, then, a familiar type of composure that creates an appearance of self-possession, based on a kind of psychosomatic dissociation. The mind creates a distance in the self—often in the form of an irony—from its own desire, from the affective core of the self, and manages, by the same token, a distance from everybody else. A sometimes compelling but ambiguous aura, by communicating a relative absence of neediness, renders the other dispensable. And this is done partly through projection; at its most extreme, the neediness is evoked in the other people around and then treated with sadistic dismay, as though it were an obnoxious stranger. Hell is not other people but one's need for other people.

The precocious mind in its struggle for composure is sustained by a militant fantasy of self-sufficiency, in which desire for the other is interpreted as concession to the other, a concession to possible misrecognition—misrecognition as appropriation—that most primitive, that most essentially perplexing form of power. In the child's early life the problem becomes that although the mother has the capacity to recognize the need of her infant, she exhibits a relative incapacity to do this in any reliable way. For her own good reasons she too often puts her desire in place of the infant's desire, and early states of excitement and quiescence, instead of being met as such by the mother, go unreciprocated or unacknowledged. An accumulation of such misleading experiences prompts a precocious mental development designed to make the child self-satisfying. This is what Winnicott calls "the over-growth of the mental function reactive to erratic mothering."[5]

"In the development of every individual," Winnicott writes, "the mind has a root . . . in the need of the individual, at the core of the self, for a perfect environment." *Perfect,* of course, is a word that psychoanalysis has ironized, though the pun on *root* here leads us in different directions. What Winnicott means here by "the perfect environment" is, I think, a state of virtual mutuality of recognition and desire that would make possible the child's and the parent's optimal development. But Winnicott idealizes here the wish to be understood; because the other thing that the child is always trying to reestablish in his own eyes— and that always already exists—is his own opaqueness. Composure, like a dare, sustains and challenges the idea of accurate recognition. (Winnicott's notion of the True Self instates the possibility of accurate recognition by giving it a target; this is the tautology that sustains the terms). So from Winnicott's point of view, one function of the precocious mind is to maintain composure while protecting, in fantasy, the desiring self that seeks such recognition. The desiring self is isolated by the dread of being undermined by the misrecognition of the other. The composure is organized to preclude the repetition of this experience of traumatic, exploitative, seduction of the affective core of the self, of the ordinary self that is deeply unenchanted by the spurious forms of its own specialness.

The quest for the perfect environment through the self-holding and self-hiding of composure, at its most excessive, insulates the individual from ever allowing the recognition he seeks. As Georg Groddeck, the great master of psychosomatic caricature, once wrote, "There are strange courses in life, some of which look like circles."[6]

- 5 -

Worrying and
Its Discontents

If I can think of it, it isn't what I want.
  Randall Jarrell, "The Sick Child"

A boy of ten was referred to me because of his general despondency at school. His teachers described him as having become, in the last few months, "preoccupied and sad." During an interview his mother said that he seemed to have a lot of worries but wouldn't always tell her what they were; sometimes he determinedly kept them to himself. She was genuinely bemused, and once alone with him I found something in this boy's distracted manner that distracted me. Intending to say "What are the worries?" I in fact said to him, "What are worries?" Quite naturally puzzled by the question, he thought for a moment, then replied triumphantly, "Farts that don't work," and blushed. I said, "Yes, some farts are worth keeping." He grinned and said, "Treasure."

For this boy worrying was a way of holding on to something, a form of storage. It transpired from our conversations that worries were like gifts he kept for his mother, and he was fearful of running out of them. What better gift to give to one's mother—especially if she was unsure of herself—than a worry she could resolve and so feel fully empowered as a good mother? He told me that he frequently dreamed of "rooms full of the heads of big game on the walls," and it was clear from his associations that he had conceived a scenario in which one day he would give his mother his complete collection of trophies, all his best worries. With remarkable economy he was using worries both to look after his mother—giving her something, one day, to make her feel better—and to seduce the oedipal mother of desire with irresistible invitations that were proof of his potency. He was, in short, as we both soon realized, very worried about losing his worries. If he did, he might have to use another part of his body—alluded to by the heads in the dream and how they got on the wall—to engage an object. From a psychoanalytic perspective it is the patient's need for the symptom, despite his paradoxical invitation to the analyst to help rid him of it, that radically revises any conventional notions of cure. After all, what would he be thinking about if he wasn't worrying?

The description of worries as "farts that don't work" raises, by implication, the question of what kind of work it is imagined that farts are supposed to be doing. (It's worth noting that one of this boy's manifest symptoms was an inability to work.) If, in this boy's view, worries are farts that don't work, what is the equivalent in mental life of farts that do work? Farts are often intimations of things to come, hints or bulletins from an internal somatic process that can be beyond omnipotent control, and in most contexts they are socially inappropriate reminders of this process. So a fart that doesn't work is a portent of nothing; it does not disclose a necessary process under way. And it isn't disruptive; it produces no change in the surrounding atmosphere. It is a thwarted internal experience rather than an exchange between inner and outer. If we take the kind of biological analogy familiar in Kleinian theory from Wilfred Bion's work, we can say that thinking something through can be described as metabolizing or digesting emotional experience.[1] For this boy, then, worrying could be a form of emotional constipation, an unproductive mental process that got him nowhere; and this was part of its value to him. Like all symptoms, from a psychoanalytic point of view, it was among other things an attempt to arrest the passing of time. Auden reported a well-known Icelandic proverb, "Every man loves the smell of his own farts." Not everyone, though, loves the smell of his own thoughts, perhaps because they reek of change.

To approach the ordinary subject of worrying, it is useful,

from a developmental point of view, to remember that we are "worried about" before we begin to worry. Being worried about is both one of the oppressions and one of the reassurances of childhood. Potentially a threat, "I'm worried about you" continues into adult life as an accusation and a claim. But it is a crucial constituent of the infant's and child's life to be able to evoke concern and interest, to have another person available to worry about him. What we think of in psychoanalysis as a symptom is often in children a way of making someone worry and therefore of making someone think. Winnicott writes, for example, of the "nuisance-value" of the symptom.[2] The parent's worry can signify a hidden preoccupation in the child, a loss of contact through a breakdown of understanding and an excess of pain. In adolescence we see a different stage of this in the use of what can be called symptoms—but are often bemusing forms of privacy—to get out of the parents' orbit even while maintaining sufficient contact with it. Parents keep the necessary link alive through worrying. It is curious, in this light, that worrying tends almost always to be talked of pejoratively. It may be part of our terror of dependency that we never hear anyone described as a good worrier.

We were once, even if we are not now, the object of someone else's worry. And, clearly, the way one was worried about—the quality of the worry we received—will to some extent be reflected in the way one worries about oneself. In object-relations theory, worrying can cover the whole spectrum from ordinary self-care to a thwarted conversation with an unlocatable object. How one uses other people in the process of worrying—to whom one tells what, and when, or whether one keeps one's worries to oneself—will be a repetition, with variations, of earlier relationships or transactions with objects. In other words, what worries are used for—what kind of medium of exchange or currency they become in one's relationship with other people and oneself—may be as revealing as what prompts them. (The question may not be "What are you worried about?" but "Whom is this worry for?") What one finds preying on one's mind, or rather, what worries are made of, may be related to what and for whom they are made. It is, of course, easy to forget that worries are imaginative creations, small epics of personal failure and anticipated catastrophe. They are, that is to say, made up. And like inverted masturbation fantasies, they are among our most intimate inventions. It is almost as though we recognize ourselves too well, are perhaps overly familiar with ourselves, as worriers. Indeed, one's own personal history of worrying—the subjects chosen, their modification over time, the people involved, the relative pain and pleasure of the experience—all this would seem to be a potentially lucid revelation of character. But Freud, of course, made us unusually suspicious of the foreground; and worries, when they are there, crowd to the front of the stage.

> Don't worry; it may never happen.
>
> Traditional saying

We can be both the subjects and the objects of our own worries. Worrying, like being concerned, preoccupied, or absorbed— but unlike dreaming, thinking, or feeling—can be done to us, according to ordinary usage. I can say, "It worries me" and also "I am worried about something." I can say "I dreamed about something"—although this, as we shall see, is different—but not as perhaps I should, "It dreams me." So in relation to my worries I can be—in the language of a traditional mystification—both active and passive. I can be their victim and I can try to master them. Worries, unlike dreams, thoughts, and feelings, are something to which we give agency. We can, with the irony that characterizes the defenses, allow them to be beyond omnipotent control, whereas for dreams we claim authorship. We can be worried, but we can't be dreamed.

The history of the word *worrying* is itself revealing. Deriving from the Old English *wyrgan*, meaning to kill by strangulation, it was originally a hunting term, describing what dogs did to their prey as they caught it. The *Oxford English Dictionary* has, among several meanings from the fourteenth to the early nineteenth century: "To swallow greedily or to devour . . . to choke a person or animal with a mouthful of food . . . to seize by the throat with the teeth and tear or lacerate; to kill or injure by biting or shaking. Said, e.g., of dogs or wolves attacking sheep, or of hounds when they seize their prey." Johnson's *Dictionary* of 1755 has for *worry:* "To tear or mangle as a beast tears it prey. To harass or persecute brutally." A worrier for Johnson is someone who persecutes others, "one who worries or torments them." Two things are immediately striking in all of this. First there is the original violence of the term, the way it signifies the vicious but successful outcome of pursuing an object of desire. This sense of brutal foreplay is picked up in Dryden's wonderful lines in *All for Love:* "And then he grew familiar with her hand / Squeezed it, and worry'd it with ravenous kisses." Worrying, then, is devouring, a peculiarly intense, ravenous form of eating. The second striking thing is that worrying, until the nineteenth century, is something one does to somebody or something else. In other words, at a certain point in history worrying became something that people could do to themselves. Using, appropriately enough, an analogy from hunting, worrying becomes a consuming, or rather self-consuming, passion. What was once thought of as animal becomes human, indeed all too human. What was once done by the mouths of the rapacious, the desirous, is now done, often with a relentless weariness, by the minds of the troubled.

It is not until the early nineteenth century, a time of significant social transformation, that we get the psychological sense of worrying as something that goes on inside someone, what the *O.E.D.* calls "denoting a state of mind," giving as illustration a quotation from Hazlitt's *Table Talk:* "Small pains are . . . more within our reach: we can fret and worry ourselves about them." Domestic agitation replaces any sense of quest in Hazlitt's essay "On Great and Little Things." By the 1850s we find many of Dickens' characters worrying or "worriting." Where once wild or not-so-wild animals had worried their prey, we find Dickens' people worrying their lives away about love and money and social status. From, perhaps, the middle of the nineteenth century people began to prey on themselves in a new kind of way. Worry begins to catch on as a description of a new state of mind. It is now impossible to imagine a life without worry. In little more than a century worrying has become what we call a fact of life, as integral to our lives, as apparently ahistorical, as any of our most familiar feelings. So in Philip Roth's recent fictional autobiography, *The Facts*, it is surprising to find the word made interesting again in the narrator's description of his hard-working Jewish father: "Despite a raw emotional nature that makes him prey to intractable worry, his life has been distinguished by the power of resurgence." The pun on *prey* suggests the devotion of that generation of American Jew to a new God. But the narrator also implies that his father's nature and history make him subject to his own persecution in the form of relentless worrying, and also that something about his life is reflected in the quality of his worry, its intractability, its obstinate persistence. A new kind of heroic resilience is required to deal with the worries of everyday life.

Even in this most cursory bit of philology we find *worry* as pursuit and persecution, two things that in psychoanalysis tend to be associated with desire. But *worrying*, as the word is used now, is manifestly countererotic; no one says "I had a really erotic worry last night," or indeed thinks of himself worrying his loved one's hands with kisses. In A. S. Byatt's novel *Still Life* one of the heroines is propositioned on a French train by a Frenchman, who offers her a "taste of Cointreau, Grand Marnier, Chartreuse" in his sleeping compartment. "Frederica replied brightly that that would be very agreeable. This was despite a strong sense that the man was unduly anxious about the outcome of his overture: anxiety is a great destroyer of response, and Frederica had no taste for being closed in a sleeping compartment with a worried man." The strong sense here is that worrying is a form of insulation, that in the excess of worry something in the proposition, to the young heroine's relief, is retracted. But Byatt alerts us to a distinction between anxiety and worrying that she cannot make. As in the seduction, something is implied and glossed over at the same time. The distinction we tend to make is that worry always has an object, that worrying is beyond displacement, whereas one can feel anxious without knowing what the anxiety is about.

Interestingly, *anxious,* which we may think of as a nineteenth-century medical term, is in its conventional psychological sense an older word than *worrying.* The *O.E.D.* offers a seventeenth-century meaning of *anxious* as "troubled or uneasy in mind about some uncertain event; being in painful or disturbing suspense; concerned; solicitous." *Anxiety,* of course, immediately found a place in the language of psychoanalysis, while *worrying* still has not. It has been subsumed by, or implicitly included in, a broad range of psychoanalytic categories, from obsessionality to phobic terrors. And this despite the rather obvious point that most adults who speak English come for psychoanalytic treatment because, in their own words, they are "worried about" something. The children I see clinically are referred because someone, quite explicitly, is worried about them. It is worth wondering, I think, given that psychoanalysis is essentially a theory of censorship, why certain words that come to mind for patients are excluded by psychoanalytic theorist; or why there need be any disparity between the language of analysts and patients. Depression, for example, has been the subject of extensive psychoanalytic speculation, but not sadness; mania has been accounted for theoretically, but not the intense pleasure of erotic excitement. It is a fact that no one worries in the Bible—the word does not occur—but it seems peculiar that the word cannot be found in the index of the *Standard Edition* of Freud's work.

> I have a life without latent content.
>
> Alexander Portnoy

In beginning to consider the worrying of everyday life as the product of an extreme form of secondary revision—a worry, that is to say, as a stifled, indeed an overprotected dream—it may be useful to remember the possible implications of the etymology of the word itself. After all, even spurious etymologies were once a respectable source of psychoanalytic speculation. When we worry, then, what are we trying to eat? What is there to pursue or get rid of? How does one hunt for something in oneself—or, more ominously, prey on oneself—and what would it mean to devour what one caught? We are familiar with the notion of worrying away at a problem, like a dog gnawing a bone, but is it absurd to suggest that we are doing a kind of violence to ourselves when we worry? Worrying can, for example, be an aggression, a critique turned against the self. When we lie awake at night worrying, there may be a dream we are trying not to have. Certainly people are more often starved of dreams than of worries. And the ordinary worry that projects a catastrophe into the future can easily be seen as the equivalent in consciousness of what Freud called punishment dreams, which "merely replace the forbidden wish-fulfilment by the appropriate punishment for it: that is to say, they fulfil the wish of the sense of guilt which is the reaction to the repudiated impulse."[3] Worries, then, can be punishments for wishes, or wishes cast in persecutory form; in the familiar act of worrying we may wish to avert the catastrophe and also to precipitate it. Flirting with possibilities, we are both the hunter and the hunted. There are, one could say elaborating Freud's phrase, those wrecked by success, and those wrecked by anticipating failure; or rather, those apparently wrecked by the wish to fail or the fear of success. Even if worrying is a covert critique of the fantasies of success in the culture, it is clear that worrying has an equivocal relationship with the wishing that in Freud's view dominates mental life.

The unconscious, Freud writes, "consists of wishful impulses. These instinctual impulses are co-ordinate with one another . . . and are exempt from mutual contradiction . . . There are in this system no negation, no doubt, no degrees of certainty."[4] Since worrying by definition implies conflict, we must infer that the unconscious doesn't, so to speak, have any worry in it. We have to imagine, according to Freud, that there is a part of ourselves that has nothing to worry about, that is exempt from this most persistent form of self-doubt. Worrying, like dreaming, is born of conflict, and therefore of censorship. It involves the compromise of representation and derives from instinctual wishes. But the dream-work that Freud described is ingenious in its transformation of the forbidden into the sufficiently acceptable. Compared with the dream, the worry is almost pure, uncooked day-residue; indeed, it is addicted to reality. There is apparently little condensation or displacement; there seems to be no question of intelligibility, although there is a noticeable intensity of feeling. Worrying, that is to say, often has the appearance, the screen, that we associate with a certain version of reality.

Compared with the extraordinary invention of the dream, the ordinary worry seems drab. As remote as possible from the forbidden, the worry, unlike the dream, is part of the routine, the predictability of everyday life. A moment's thought will tell us what, if anything, we have to worry about tomorrow. No amount of thinking will tell us what we will dream tonight. All of us may be surrealists in our dreams, but in our worries we are incorrigibly bourgeois. It may be worth considering, then, a glib Freudian paradox: that some of the most efficient forms of censorship are those that render themselves invisible. How would one begin, or bother, to think that a shopping list or a telephone directory was a product of censorship? To worry about one's health, or about one's children, about money, or being late, or losing one's job, is not in any obvious sense enigmatic or puzzling. And yet it may be one of the functions of worrying to cramp and contain—to overorganize—more imaginatively elaborate or even violent responses to such very real predicaments. As a furtive protest, worrying is an attempt at simplification. It can give a local habitation and a name to a diversity of grievance and desire. A worry, one could say, is a muted dream, an overprotection of the self. But one could feel baffled, indeed radically misrecognized, if one's ordinary worries were interpreted as a Freudian analyst might interpret a dream. There is no obvious reason, though, why our associations to any of the elements in a worry should not be revealing.

It may not be the dream that is the royal road to the unconscious, but the style of interpretation it makes possible.

Nevertheless, from a psychoanalytic perspective, "What did you dream about?" and "What are you worried about?" are quite different kinds of questions. The answers to them confront us with our assumptions about interpretation—both what is subject to what we call interpretation and what, in the form of interpretation, we might pertinently say. Clearly, the demand, or invitation, in the answers to these questions are different. And when we answer the question "What are you worried about?" we, in a recognizable sense, mean what we say; we have conviction about what we are referring to. But when I say that I dreamed about a green cat last night, I am giving a true report, yet we can assume that a process of substitution, of symbolization, has been in play. We infer that work has been done on the stuff of emotional life, that there is an overnight history of transformation that opens into a vast unconscious personal history, whereas worrying seems like a reaction to and not a reworking of our experience. By binding us to the present and the future it abolishes the past that is, so to speak, behind this particular piece of worrying, that existed prior to its appearance as a preoccupation. It seals time by encapsulating a sequence. When we worry, we look forward but are not tempted to look very far back. We are dutiful in the way Orpheus should have been.

Worrying implies a future, a way of looking forward to things. It is a conscious conviction that a future exists, one in which something terrible might happen, which is of course ultimately true. So worrying is an ironic form of hope. But dreams are always set in the past, both in Freud's sense of their being the disguised fulfillment of a repressed infantile wish and in the more verifiable sense that you cannot, by definition, ask someone what he is dreaming because a dream is always a retrospective report, never the so-called thing-in-itself. And always the question "What did you dream?" in its most straightforward sense is notoriously difficult to answer. The dream, or perhaps the dreaming subject, "fades," as Lacan puts it, when the dreamer awakens. The dreaming subject is even more elusive—almost impossible to construct—than his or her product, the dream. "Who is dreaming?" is clearly a less ludicrous question than "Who is worrying?"

What people do to their dreams effortlessly—that is, forget them—people have to try to do to their worries. To remember a worry is as easy as to forget a dream. Worries are present and tend to recur, and we are manifestly present in them. They show a coherent subject in an intelligible, if unsettling, narrative; they assume a pragmatic self bent on problem-solving, not an incurably desiring subject in the disarray of not knowing what he wants. We use worries to focus and are prone to use them to simulate purpose (just as when we are intimidated by possibility). When people describe a known task—passing an exam, paying a debt, being cured of an illness—they do not seem to allude to an unlocatable lack or, more absurdly, a certain death. As an integral part of a familiar internal environment, these specific worries can be very reassuring because they preempt what is in actuality an unknowable future. The worst thing that could happen is more comforting than the unimaginable thing.

Worrying tacitly constitutes a self—or, at least, a narrator—by assuming the existence of one; for how could there be a worry without a worrier? It is, of course, difficult to imagine a dream without a dreamer, but also to know what the dreamer looks like. A worrier has, so to speak, a familiar face; the iconography of the dreaming self is nowhere to be found. And it is exactly in this elusive area of inquiry that worrying focuses a contemporary dilemma in psychoanalysis. In what could, broadly speaking, be called object-relations theory, we have potentially guaranteed subjects or selves in relation to potentially knowable and facilitating objects in search of personal development through intimacy. A modernized Freudian, on the other hand, can easily see the self as merely a function of representation—where else is it except in its descriptions?—in a world of comparably oblique objects. Here fantasies of growth or purpose conceal the impossibility, the unexorcizable

lack, at the heart of being. Relationships, in this view, are necessarily ironized, because although they are essential to survival,
the persistence of desire prefigures defeat. Desire implies a lack
that no object can appease. Worrying, in this kind of arena,
looks silly. It seems to lack metaphysical ambition. But from
an object-relations point of view we could say that worrying
prepares the self, at best in collaboration with responsive others.
And we could also say that potentially, through refusing the
benefit of others, worrying impoverishes the self by attacking
the possibility of its imaginative modification. As a medium of
exchange, then, worrying regulates intimacy, and it is often an
appropriate response to ordinary demands that begin to feel
excessive. But from a modernized Freudian view, worrying—
as a reflex response to demand—never puts the self or the
objects of its interest into question, and that is precisely its
function in psychic life. It domesticates self-doubt.

If we adapt Wittgenstein's famous question "Is belief an
experience?" to the matter in hand and ask "Is worrying an
experience?" we are left more empty-handed than we may want
to be.[5] If we were anthropologists who had discovered a tribe
that engaged in a pervasive activity they called worrying, how
would we go about getting a sense of what they meant? I seem
to know when I'm worried—I recognize the signs—but this in
itself can preclude my finding out what I'm doing when I
worry. The tendentious comparison with dreaming reveals, I
think, how worrying sets limits to the kind of curiosity we can
have about it. We can think about thinking, but perhaps we
don't worry enough about worrying. If worrying is, say, a
defense against dreaming, if the worry is the contrived, conscious alternative to the dream, at the opposite end of some
imaginary spectrum, then there may also be something,
paradoxically, that they have in common. They both incorpo-
rate reality to defeat interpretation, and they do not always
succeed.

Returning the Dream:
In Memoriam Masud Khan

No bird soars too high, if he soars with his own wings.
William Blake, "The Marriage of Heaven and Hell"

Always, in the patient as in the analyst, there is a repertoire of fantasies of what, it is assumed, the object can do for the subject; or what, in Winnicott's language, the object can eventually be used for. But the fantasies—where the subject, of course, is fluent in the work of wishing—are mostly unconscious. And yet object-relations theory provides us with something we could never find in Freud: a veritable catalogue of objects, a series of texts that constitute a dramatis personae of facilitators and saboteurs. Belief in the object—and here we must exclude Klein—tends to displace Freud's doubts about the subject. "Childhood love is boundless," he writes in his elegy for desire, "It demands exclusive possession, it is not content with less than all. But it has a second characteristic: it has, in point of fact, no aim and is incapable of obtaining complete satisfaction; and principally for that reason it is doomed to end in disappointment."[1] It is this notorious second characteristic that puts childhood love beyond the pleasure principle, beyond the repetition compulsion and beyond the object.

For Freud, then, excess and aimlessness; and for Winnicott, holding and the developmental process. There is, in Winnicott's work, as in Khan's, a promising sense of the object's potential. A latent teleology of the Self displaces an unavoidable division in the subject. It is the quality of mothering, and not the unconscious per se, that is the source of strangeness, that can promote obstacles to intimacy. But in Winnicott's work the early intimacy of the mother and her infant is always there in service of—cocooning, as it were—an essentially strange and solitary True Self; strange by virtue of having no wish to be known. "At the centre of each person," he writes, "is an incommunicado element and this is sacred and most worthy of preservation."[2] Interestingly, Winnicott uses an un-English word, *incommunicado,* for his most sacred idea. But there is, as we know, in Winnicott's work, a negative theology of the Self. In the context of psychoanalysis as a hermeneutics it is difficult not to hear this "permanently noncommunicating" element, like the fabled "silence of God," as offering us a powerful message; but of what and for whom, of course, it is impossible to say. Winnicott makes this impossibility of knowing quite clear. There is an excess here, not of childhood love, but of silence: an always occulted aim, but not aimlessness. It is the acknowledgment of what cannot be known, but only protected—"preserved," as Winnicott puts it—that defines nurture for Winnicott. The aim of intimacy is to sponsor the solitary unknowability of the True Self.

It is only the impingement of the mother, in Winnicott's view, that compels the infant and the child to use the various strategies of self-estrangement that he calls the False Self. The False Self manages the imposed illusion of the mother—or sometimes the analyst's theoretical preoccupations—those demands that are extrinsic to development, while the True Self lives in seclusion awaiting the good object. The object, in Winnicott as in Khan, has a benign potential for noninterference. So in Khan's case histories we find, whatever the symptomatology, a remarkable phenomenological subtlety moving inevitably, it seems, toward a reconstruction of a failure of the holding environment. There is no sense, as there is in Freud, that the constitution of the human subject entails a holding environment that is a failure; that the world is never good enough for us. A feeling of being strange in a malign sense, of being radically other to oneself, could be symptomatic only of what Khan calls, à propos of Artaud, "the sickness of the self-system."[3] After all, what is the transitional object if not the impossibility—or the refusal—of the Uncanny?

In its twilight, the British Empire produced a theory of good-enough mothering as the antithesis, the guilty critique, of what was always a bad-enough imperialism. Throughout Khan's work there is a continual and passionate critique of the overinterpretative analyst as maternal saboteur, as the one who appropriates or colonizes the patient, demanding "exclusive possession." His return to Freud involved a certain reserve about the analyst as interpreter. "I believe that today, once again," he writes, "we have to start, as Freud did in 1895, by giving a true phenomenological account of our clinical encounter with our patients, without paralysing the ambiguities of the therapeutic exchange by coercing them into the straitjacket of our metapsychological preconceptions."[4] Much of Khan's work seeks to clarify the nature of the demand in the analyst's interpretation. Each psychoanalytic theorist, as we know, makes a new kind of demand on the patient. And it is this which the patient will either have to manage or be able to use. (It can, of course, be the very obscurity of the demand that is mutative for the patient.)

So there is also, in Khan's work, by the same token, an insistent preoccupation with, and attempt at, redescribing the analytic situation based on Winnicott's model of the mother-infant relationship. The analyst's project becomes—and this is one of Winnicott's distinctive contributions, elaborated by Khan—the establishing of a reliable setting to facilitate and sponsor an innate developmental process. Unobtrusively attentive, the analyst is careful, in Khan's words, not to "initiate a reactive as-if dialogue between the analyst and the patient, from which the person of the patient can stay absent forever."[5] But if it is possible for a person to engage in a dialogue in which he can stay absent for ever, there is also one place in which he is always present, in his dreams. "For whom is the dream dreamed?" is a quite different question from "For whom is the dialogue spoken?" "The use of dreams in analysis," Freud wrote, "is something very remote from their original aim."[6] One could not, presumably, say the same thing about the use of language.

For Khan, unlike Winnicott, as a complement to the analogy of the analytic setting with the mother–infant relationship, there is also—articulated in three papers that constitute a series (1962, 1972, 1976)[7]—a description of the analytic setting as comparable, optimally, to the preconditions for dreaming. "Freud intuitively recreated," Khan writes, "a physical and psychic ambience in the analytic setting which corresponds significantly to that intrapsychic state in the dreamer which is conducive to a 'good dream.'"[8] But how does an intrapsychic model work for what is essentially an intersubjective experience, and where does this place the analyst? What kind of sense can we make of the so-called one-body relationship—of "the infant-in-care alone with himself"—as a paradigm for the interpretative practice that is psychoanalysis? It is, as we shall see, part of Khan's intention to return the dream to the dreamer, to ensure its fullness of meaning—its "eloquence," in J.-B. Pontalis' term[9]—through minimal translation.

For Freud, the problem posed by the object was that it could only frustrate; for Khan, the problem posed by the object is that it always demands.

> One's real life is so often the life that one does not lead.
>
> Oscar Wilde, *L'Envoi to Rose-Leaf and Apple-Leaf*

It is in relation to the dream that Khan begins to describe the kind of object, or object-relation, that increasingly preoccupies him (object-relations is, so to speak, novelistic in its continual invention of new "characters"). And it is the inverse of this particular object-relation that he finds in perversion; because in perversion there is the refusal, the terror, of strangeness—strangeness as signifying difference—in the subtle simulation of intimacy. The pervert, in Khan's version, parodies—or rather, attacks—solitary states of unknowing and imaginative elaboration through compulsive action with an accomplice; and this is done to mask psychic pain. The accomplice is, by definition, the antitype of this new kind of object, one of whose functions is to hold psychic pain, but simply by acknowledging it, and not to collude in its denial—one collusion being the assumption that it is interpretable, that it can be made into into something else. So another function of this new object in the analytic situation is to set those limits to knowing that "provide coverage for the patient's self-experience in the clinical situation"[10]—and by "coverage" here Khan means ego-support—with the analyst functioning as what he calls an "auxiliary ego." The pervert, however—or rather, someone who uses at any given moment a perverse solution—denies that there is anything new to know. This can, of course, have its heuristic advantages, since every denial makes possible another kind of acknowledgment (just as each insight is the product of a specific blindness). But there is, as Khan intimates, a complicated relationship between what in psychoanalysis is called perversion and the notion, so dear to the British School, of "not-knowing." Indeed one could describe the work of Winnicott, Khan, and Marion Milner as the attempt to find a viable alternative to perversion, a new model for theory. Because perversions are always prefigurings; or, to put it another way, we could say that we are being perverse whenever we think we know beforehand exactly what we desire. To know beforehand is to assume that otherness, whether it be a person, a medium, an environment, is redundant; that it has nothing to offer us, that it brings nothing—or just rage and disappointment—to the occasion. For Khan, I think, the so-called pervert, in his apparent knowingness, was an implicit parody of a certain kind of analyst.

Derived from Winnicott's formative paper, "The Capacity to Be Alone" (1958)—in which, it should be noted, there is no mention of the self and in which it is announced in silence, as it were, that there is a constitutive difference between the notion of presence and the idea of the self—this new object, in the guise of the analyst, allows himself to be used by the patient in a way that increasingly, for Khan, begins to define the analytic encounter. The mother, in the scenario Winnicott describes in his paper, does not correspond to an interpreter but is, as it were, a presence available for comment, should it be required: a "witness," to use Khan's ambiguous term, holding the situation through her known potential for availability, not through her vigilance or intent curiosity. Only then can the infant be alone in the presence of someone. Like a more relaxed version of the censor in the dream-work, the mother's presence makes possible the crystallization of the infant's desire without rupture—of sleep in the case of the dreamer, and of ego-function in the case of the child. The mother cannot create desire, conjure it into being; she can only provide the conditions in which it is possible. She can allow what Winnicott calls, vis-à-vis the spatula game, "the full course of an experience." Desire, like the dream, cannot be arranged, but (unlike the Proustian epiphany) the setting for its possibility can be provided. What can be understood, what constitutes the object of knowledge—and this is the paradox that Khan will present us with—are the preconditions, the form, the setting, but not the product, not the reported dream. As with the transitional object, there is a sense in which it does not matter what the dream happens to be; what is significant is that it has happened—that it could be dreamed— and then how it is used. From "Dream Psychology and the Evolution of the Psychoanalytic Situation" (1962), through "The Use and Abuse of Dream in Psychic Experience" (1972), to "Beyond the Dreaming Experience" (1976), we see a curious process intimated in the repeated use of that extraordinary English word—with, it should be added, a history that is always occluded in its use in British psychoanalysis—*experience*. There is, as we read Khan's writing on dreams, a gradual attenuation of the idea of the dream as text, and therefore of the analyst's role in relation to the dream as primarily interpretative; indeed, a growing sense in Khan's work that to speak is always to be spoken for.

The dream as text, and therefore as available for interpretation, is replaced by the dream as experience, formative by virtue of being unknowable. The dream becomes a virtual synecdoche for the True Self of the patient, who is not an object to be deciphered. Dreams become bulletins of the developmental process signifying the silent metabolism of the Self. It is only when the developmental process is felt to go wrong that the idea of a developmental process is useful. "We should no longer say,"

Vincent Descombes writes, vis-à-vis the problem of what he calls "the escape of meaning" in hermeneutics, "I have understood, but have I understood correctly or am I mistaken / deceived? But rather, I have understood, but was it possible to understand?"[11] What could be more pertinent to that tantalizing hermeneutic object, the dream?

If the dream, as Freud showed, is the way we tell ourselves secrets at night about our desire, it also represents the impenetrable privacy of the Self. "A person in his dreaming experience," Khan writes, "can actualise aspects of the self that perhaps never become overtly available to his introspection or his dreams."[12] The dreamer, we can say, is present in experience but absent in knowledge. And it is the so-called dreaming experience of the patient, like the waking ego of the patient, from which the analyst is excluded. We may wonder, from a different point of view, where this dreaming experience resides if not in language. After all, representations are always outside. Clearly, there cannot be a private language; but there can be a sense, Khan implies, conveyed in language, of a person's irreducible privacy. The dreaming experience comes to signify that which is beyond description in the total *vécu* of the patient.

If, as Khan claims with his extravagant virtuosity, "The dreaming subject is the entire subject,"[13] then pathology is whatever in the person's history has sabotaged—and here we find the use of reconstruction and therefore the use of the analyst—the person's potential for dreaming experience. A person has to be in the dream of himself before he can dream. The analyst's aim is to facilitate and establish, through holding, the dream-space in the patient where experience can unfold. As the interpreter, he simply helps build the stage, as it were, for a good dream. As interpreter of the dream-text itself, he is a latecomer in the process that brings with it its own guarantee. Freud, as Khan notes, had intimated something of this in his cryptic remark, "those dreams best fulfil their function about which one knows nothing after waking."[14] It was the dream, Freud said, not only the interpreted dream, that was the royal road to the unconscious.

I am there from where no news even of myself reaches me.

Persian aphorism

In his first paper on the subject of the dream, Khan makes it clear that the capacity for the "good dream," akin to the capacity to use the analytic transference, depends ultimately on the patient's experience in infancy of states of sufficient satisfaction. Freud, he writes, "makes it quite explicit that wish-fulfilment in dreams is only possible if the mnemic images of the previous satisfaction of needs are available for cathexis," [15] and he links this with Winnicott's account of infant care. In "The Use and Abuse of Dream in Psychic Experience," there is an emerging sense of the dream capacity as facilitated by environmental provision, and dream-space seen as the intrapsychic equivalent of transitional space where a person "actualises certain types of experiences." [16] The dream-space contains, for the purpose of personal elaboration, what might otherwise be acted out—or rather, evacuated—in what Khan calls "social space." But Khan is careful to differentiate the experiences actualized in the dream-space from the dream as "symbolic mental creation" (he will conclude the final paper in the series by stating unequivocally, "There is a dreaming experience to which the dream text holds no clue"). [17] The analyst's interpretation does not so much translate unconscious content as show the patient, with the help of associations, what he has used the dream-space for.

Transitional phenomena—unlike the "impersonal object" that Khan suggests the pervert "puts . . . between his desire and his accomplice" and that alienates the pervert from himself and the object of desire[18]—are integral to the process of personalization. The aim of any interpretation is to facilitate the personalization of the dream. And the dream, like all transitional phenomena, is conveying the patient to an unknowable destination. Like the mother who plays in the transitional space—a space, Khan insists, always vulnerable to preemptive intrusion—the analyst is there to sustain the experience. A clinical preoccupation with "how to let oneself be used, become the servant of a process" [19] implies that interpretation might become a sophisticated form of interruption, the way the analyst insists on being important.

In "Beyond the Dreaming Experience" (1976), which should perhaps be titled "Beyond the Interpreting Experience," there is, as a consequence, a disillusionment with the very object that Freud placed at the beginning of the psychoanalytic enterprise—the remembered dream or dream-text. It is not now "the component parts of the dream-text," those parts Freud encouraged us to dissect, but "the whole dream as an experiential entity "that has become the focus of interest, because the "dreaming experience," in Khan's view, bears no necessary relation to the dream-text. "The dreaming experience," he writes, "is an entirety that actualises the self in an unknowable way . . . dreaming itself is beyond interpretation."[20] The statement, in absolute terms, invites intuitive assent, but we may also want to ask, how does he know? Or perhaps a more psychoanalytic question, strictly speaking, would be, what is the wish that is satisfied by believing this to be true?

This disillusionment with the dream-text—and, by implication, with the analyst as controller of the hermeneutic—signifies Khan's distrust of psychoanalysis as epistemology, as a theater of the epistemophilic instinct that Klein was so impressed by. For what is the developmental process if not a limit set to—or a defiance of—the Other's claim to knowledge about the Self, that elusiveness staged as an essence, but always incommunicado? And whose version of self-knowledge, despite psychoanalysis, does not sound glib? Khan's work, with its generous skepticism, is an acknowledgment—necessarily ironized in a secular culture—that we did not invent ourselves, that we have only described ourselves.

Toward the end of his life Khan was increasingly preoccupied by "a person's relation with himself"[21]—that is, the process of personalization—and with the possible meaning of Freud's most recondite concept of primary repression. He was preoccupied, in other words, with that which was beyond the object's knowledge, but not beyond the object's acknowledgment.

"Maybe," John Wisdom wrote, "we look for too simple a likeness to what we dreamed."[22] Maybe, Khan suggests, we do not always need a likeness.

- 7 -

On Being Bored

Life, friends, is boring. We must not say so.
John Berryman, "Dream Song 14"

Children are not oracles, but they ask with persistent regularity the great existential question, "What shall we do now?" Every adult remembers, among many other things, the great ennui of childhood, and every child's life is punctuated by spells of boredom: that state of suspended anticipation in which things are started and nothing begins, the mood of diffuse restlessness which contains that most absurd and paradoxical wish, the wish for a desire.

As psychoanalysis has brought to our attention the passionate intensity of the child's internal world, it has tended to equate significance with intensity and so has rarely found a place, in theory, for all those less vehement, vaguer, often more subtle feelings and moods that much of our lives consist of. It is part of Winnicott's contribution to have alerted us to the importance, in childhood, of states of relative quiescence, of moods that could never figure, for example, in Melanie Klein's gothic melodrama of emotional development. Although there are several references in the psychoanalytic literature to the project of the boring patient, and fewer to the seemingly common adult fear of being boring, very little has been written about the child's ordinary experience of being bored, a mood that by definition seems to preclude elaborate description. As any child will tell us, it's just having nothing to do. But moods, of course, are points of view.

Clinically one comes across children unable to be bored, and more often, children unable to be anything else. In any discussion of waiting, at least in relation to the child, it makes sense to speak of boredom because the bored child is waiting, unconsciously, for an experience of anticipation. In ordinary states of boredom the child returns to the possibility of his own desire. That boredom is actually a precarious process in which the child is, as it were, both waiting for something and looking for something, in which hope is being secretly negotiated; and in this sense boredom is akin to free-floating attention. In the muffled, sometimes irritable confusion of boredom the child is reaching to a recurrent sense of emptiness out of which his real desire can crystallize. But to begin with, of course, the child needs the adult to hold, and hold to, the experience—that is, to recognize it as such, rather than to sabotage it by distraction. The child's boredom starts as a regular crisis in the child's developing capacity to be alone in the presence of the mother. In other words, the capacity to be bored can be a developmental achievement for the child.

Experiencing a frustrating pause in his usually mobile attention and absorption, the bored child quickly becomes preoccupied by his lack of preoccupation. Not exactly waiting for someone else, he is, as it were, waiting for himself. Neither hopeless nor expectant, neither intent nor resigned, the child is in a dull helplessness of possibility and dismay. In simple terms the child always has two concurrent, overlapping projects: the project of self-sufficiency in which use of, and need for, the other is interpreted, by the child, as a concession; and a project of mutuality that owns up to a dependence. In the banal crisis of boredom, the conflict between the two projects is once again renewed. Is it not, indeed revealing, what the child's boredom evokes in the adults? Heard as a demand, sometimes as an accusation of failure or disappointment, it is rarely agreed to, simply acknowledged. How often, in fact, the child's boredom is met by that most perplexing form of disapproval, the adult's wish to distract him—as though the adults have decided that the child's life must be, or be seen to be, endlessly interesting. It is one of the most oppressive demands of adults that the child should be interested, rather than take time to find what interests him. Boredom is integral to the process of taking one's time.

While the child's boredom is often recognized as an incapacity, it is usually denied as an opportunity. A precociously articulate eleven-year-old boy was referred to me because, in his mother's words, he was "more miserable than he realized," and had no friends because of his "misleading self-presentation." For several weeks, while we got to know each other, he chatted fluently in a quite happy, slightly dissociated way about his vast array of interests and occupations. The only significant negative transference occurred when he mentioned, in passing, that he might sometimes be too busy to come and see me. He was mostly in a state of what I can only describe as blank exuberance about how full his life was. As he was terrified of his own self-doubt, I asked him very few questions, and they were always tactful. But at one point, more direct than I intended to be, I asked him if he was ever bored. He was surprised by the question and replied with a gloominess I hadn't seen before in this relentlessly cheerful child, "I'm not allowed to be bored." I asked him what would happen if he allowed himself to be bored, and he paused for the first time, I think, in the treatment, and said, "I wouldn't know what I was looking forward to," and was, momentarily, quite panic-stricken by this thought. This led us, over the next year, into a discussion of what in one language would be called this boy's false self. Being good, in terms of the maternal demand, was having lots of interests, interests, that is, of a respectable, unembarrassing sort, nothing that could make him feel awkward and strong. In the course of the treatment he gradually developed in himself a new capacity, the capacity to be bored. I once suggested to him that being good was a way of stopping people knowing him, to which he agreed but added, "When I'm bored I don't know myself!"

If the bored child cannot sufficiently hold the mood, or use the adult as an unimpinging auxiliary ego, there is a premature flight from uncertainty, the familiar orgy of promiscuous and disappointing engagements that is also, as it were, a trial action in action, a trying things out. At its worst there is what the adult will come to know, from his repertoire of displacements, as the simulation of his desire, which in the child often takes the form of a regressive fabrication of need. A boy of eight referred for being "excessively greedy and always bored," said to me in the first session, "If I eat everything I won't have to eat anymore." This could have meant several things, but for him it meant then that if he could eat everything he would no longer need to be hungry. One magical solution, of course, to the problem of having been tantalized is to have no desire. For this boy greed was, among other things, an attack on the desiring part of the self, a wish to get to the end of his appetite and finish with it once and for all. Part of the total fantasy of greed is always the attempt to eat up one's own appetite. But for this desolate child greed was a form of self-cure for a malign boredom that continually placed him on the threshold of an emptiness, a lack, that he couldn't bear; an emptiness in which his own idiosyncratic, unconscious desire lurked as a possibility. When I asked him if he was ever lonely, he said that he was "too bored to be lonely."

> Inability to tolerate empty space limits the amount of space available.
>
> W. R. Bion, *Cogitations*

The child is dependent not only on the mother, but also on his desire. Both can be lost and refound. So perhaps boredom is merely the mourning of everyday life? "It is really only because we know so well how to explain it," Freud wrote of mourning, "that this attitude does not seem to us pathological." But the child's boredom is a mood that seems to negate the possibility of explanation. It is itself unexplaining, inarticulate; certainly not pathological but nevertheless somehow unacceptable. Some of the things Freud says in *Mourning and Melancholia* about the melancholic can easily be said of the bored child. "One feels . . . a loss . . . has occurred, but one cannot see clearly what it is that has been lost, and it is all the more reasonable to suppose that the patient cannot consciously perceive what he has lost either." What the bored child experiences himself as losing is "something to do" at the moment in which nothing is inviting.

"The inhibition of the melancholic seems puzzling to us," Freud writes, "because we cannot see what it is that is absorbing him so entirely." In a sense, the bored child is absorbed by his lack of absorption, and yet he is also preparing for something of which he is unaware, something that will eventually occasion an easy transition or a mild surprise of interest. "In mourning it is the world that has become poor and empty; in melancholia it is the ego itself." And in boredom, we might add, it is both. The brief but intense boredoms of childhood are reactive to no great loss, but are merely an interruption—after something and before something else. Like all genuine transitional states, their destination is unclear. Certainly when bored as an adult one cannot, in Freud's words, "hide the weakness of one's own nature."[1] But what, we might ask, following Freud's approach in this extraordinary paper, is the work which boredom performs for the child?

Winnicott, who often refers to instinctual life as a "complication," provides a way of looking at boredom in his paper "The Observation of Infants in a Set Situation" (1941), particularly with his notion of the period of hesitation, a state of preconscious surmise. In the set situation of Winnicott's consultation he asks "the mother to sit opposite me with the angle of the table coming between me and her, she sits down with the baby on her knee. As a routine I place a right-angled shining tongue-depressor at the edge of the table and I invite the mother to place the child in such a way that, if the child should wish to handle the spatula, it is possible." This sets the scene for the three stages of the infant's behavior that are to become for Winnicott a paradigm of the analytic process. The spatula, like the "good" interpretation, and even the analyst himself, is that which the patient is ready to use, that makes sense to him to use; and the setting is one in which the child "only becomes able to find his desire again in so far as his testing of the environment affords satisfactory results."[2] The bored child is waiting, without the conscious representation of an object, to find his desire again. Once again he does not know what he is looking forward to. This is Winnicott's description of part of the process:

Stage 1. The baby puts his hand to the spatula, but at this moment discovers unexpectedly that the situation must be given thought. He is in a fix. Either with his hand resting on the spatula and his body quite still he looks at me and his mother with big eyes, and watches and waits, or, in certain cases, he withdraws interest completely and buries his face in the front of his mother's blouse. It is usually possible to manage the situation so that active reassurance is not given, and it is very interesting to watch the gradual and spontaneous return of the child's interest in the spatula.

Stage 2. All the time, in "the period of hesitation" (as I call it), the baby holds his body still (but not rigid). Gradually he becomes brave enough to let his feelings develop, and then the picture changes quite quickly. The moment at which this first phase changes into the second is evident, for the child's acceptance of the reality of desire for the spatula is heralded by a change in the inside of the mouth, which becomes flabby, while the tongue looks thick and soft, and saliva flows copiously. Before long he puts the spatula into his mouth and is chewing it with his gums, or seems to be copying father smoking a pipe. The change in the baby's behaviour is a striking feature. Instead of expectancy and stillness there now develops self-confidence, and there is free bodily movement, the latter related to manipulation of the spatula.

I have frequently made the experiment of trying to get the spatula to the infant's mouth during the stage of hesitation. Whether the hesitation corresponds to my normal or differs from it in degree or quality, I find that it is impossible during this stage to get the spatula to the child's mouth apart from the exercise of brutal strength. In certain cases where the inhibition is acute any effort on my part that results in the spatula being moved towards the child produces screaming, mental distress, or actual colic.

The baby now seems to feel that the spatula is in his possession, perhaps in his power, certainly available for the purposes of self-expression.[3]

Clearly, for the bored child nothing is "available for the purposes of self-expression." Instead of "expectancy and stillness"
there is a dreary agitation; instead of "self-confidence and . . .
free bodily movement" there is a cramped restlessness. Boredom, one could say, is the set situation before there is a spatula
to be found; or perhaps, more absurdly, a set situation full of
spatulas in which the child has to find one that really appeals
to him. The bored child, a sprawl of absent possibilities, is
looking for something to hold his attention. He is like a man
who walks as quickly as possible through a gallery until a picture actually arrests his attention, until he is stopped—and at
that point, we might add, the transference has taken. For the
child to be allowed to have what Winnicott calls "the full course
of the experience" the child needs the use of an environment
that will suggest things without imposing them; not preempt
the actuality of the child's desire by force-feeding, not distract
the child by forcing the spatula into his mouth. It is a process,
Winnicott is saying, that is easily violated—although I would
say that in growing up one needs a certain flair for distraction—
and analogous to the analytic situation, in which the analyst's
interpretations offer views rather than imposing convictions. In
psychoanalysis, by definition, a militant or moralistic compe-
tence is inappropriate, merely a distraction.

The shining spatula, like Winnicott's initial squiggle, is, of
course, an invitation to the child, an offering. What Winnicott
calls the environment, though not exactly asserting itself, is at
least tentatively promising; hinting, as it were. Gradually gain-
ing interest in something that has attracted his attention, the
infant, in his period of hesitation, "becomes brave enough to
let his feelings develop." The period, wonderfully observed and
imagined by Winnicott, in which the infant begins to experience
his desire is an intrinsically problematic, difficult time. A child
described later in the paper gets asthma during the period of
hesitation. "For this child," Winnicott writes, "asthma was
associated with the moment at which there is normally hesitation, and hesitation implies mental conflict." [4] One can ask then,
adapting Freud's phrase, What are the individual's preconditions

for desire, for letting his feelings develop? What are the situations he sets—the occasions he organizes—to make desire possible? Boredom, of course, is prehesitation, but in each period of boredom the child returns to these questions.

The ordinary boredom of childhood is the benign version of what gets acted out, or acted out of, in what Winnicott calls the antisocial tendency.[5] But as adults boredom returns us to the scene of inquiry, to the poverty of our curiosity, and the simple question, What does one want to do with one's time? What is a brief malaise for the child becomes for the adult a kind of muted risk. After all, who can wait for nothing?

> Clov: Do you believe in the life to come?
> Hamm: Mine was always that.
>
> Samuel Beckett, *Endgame*

In the process of waiting for the mother the child discovers a capacity for representation as a means of deferral. Representation—fantasy—is the medium in which he desires and waits. The child can conceive of himself, as a desiring subject, in her absence, only in the space that comes between them. Optimally, with the cumulative experience of waiting for a reliable mother the child will confidently find himself as the source of possibilities; and he will be relatively unembittered by his gradual pre-oedipal disillusionment and loss of omnipotence. What Melanie Klein has described as the paranoid-schizoid position[6] may be simply an account of the state of mind of an infant who has been made to wait beyond his capacity or tolerance, to the point at which desire is experienced intrapsychically as a threat to the always precarious integrity of the ego. What Klein does reveal, following Freud, is what could be called the individual's will to substitution, the need for every absence to be a presence. For the infant, in the agonies of waiting indefinitely, the good breast turns into the bad persecuting breast, but is nevertheless present as such in the infant's mind. In Klein's developmental theory, therefore, the whole notion of waiting is being rethought because, in a sense, the infant is never alone. Without sufficient attentiveness by the mother there is to an excessive degree what Laplanche so starkly describes, in a different context, as an attack of the drives on the ego;[7] which will become, through projection, a refusal of the eventual presence of the object. It is difficult to enjoy people for whom we have waited too long. And in this familiar situation, which evokes such intensities of feeling, we wait and we try to do something other than waiting, and we often get bored—the boredom of protest that is always a screen for rage.

One can, of course, distract oneself only from what one has seen, or imagines one has seen. The defenses, as Freud described them, are forms of recognition, instruments for the compromising of knowledge. We can think of boredom as a defense against waiting, which is, at one remove, an acknowledgment of the possibility of desire. And we can use as an analogy here Freud's explanation of the double-think in fetishism from his paper of 1927. After the child has been confronted with the fact that, as he understands it, the woman lacks a penis, "we see," Freud writes, "that the perception has persisted, and that a very energetic action has been undertaken to maintain the disavowal." The child "has retained that belief but he has also given it up"; like the patient Freud mentions, he "oscillates . . . between two assumptions."[8] In boredom, we can also say, there are two assumptions, two impossible options: there is something I desire, and there is nothing I desire. But which of the two assumptions, or beliefs, is disavowed is always ambiguous, and this ambiguity accounts, I think, for the curious paralysis of boredom (it is worth remembering Joyce McDougall's sense of disavowal, that it "implies the notion of 'avowal' followed by a destruction of meaning").[9] In boredom there is the lure of a possible object of desire, and the lure of the escape from desire, of its meaninglessness.

In this context what begins for the child as the object of desire becomes, for the adult, what Christopher Bollas has described as the "transformational object." Initially the mother, it is "an object that is experientially identified by the infant with the process of the alteration of self experience." This earliest relationship becomes the precursor of, the paradigm for, "the person's search for an object (a person, place, event, ideology) that promises to transform the self." At the first stage "the mother is not yet identified as an object but is experienced as a process of transformation, and this feature remains in the trace of this object-seeking in adult life, where I believe the object is sought for its function as signifier of the process of transformation of being. Thus, in adult life, the quest is not to possess the object; it is sought in order to surrender to it as a process that alters the self."[10] But just as, for example, we cannot know beforehand which of the day's events from what Freud calls the "dream-day" will be used as day-residues in the dream-work, we cannot necessarily know what will serve as a transformational object. The fact that anything *might* serve to transform a person's life has extravagant consequences for the possible shapes of a life, and, of course, for the significance attributed to therapeutic interventions. We are drawn, in fact, to ask a brash question: a madeleine or an analyst? An analysis can at least be arranged. But it cannot, alas, organize epiphanies, or guarantee those processes of transformation—those articulations—that return the future to us through the past. Of our own past, Proust writes in *Swann's Way* (1913), "It is a labour in vain to attempt to recapture it: all the efforts of our intellect must prove futile. The past is hidden somewhere outside the realm, beyond the reach of intellect, in some material object (in the sensation which that material object will give us) which we do not suspect. And as for that object, it depends on chance whether we come upon it or not before we ourselves die."[11] The past can also, as we know, be hidden in the transference, and so can appear to be hidden in that material object called the analyst. But can we believe that there is a royal road, so to speak, to the transformational object?

Boredom, I think, protects the individual, makes tolerable for him the impossible experience of waiting for something without knowing what it could be. So the paradox of the waiting that goes on in boredom is that the individual does not know what he was waiting for until he finds it, and that often he does not know that he is waiting. One could, in this sense, speak of the "analytic attitude" as an attentive boredom. With his set of approximations the bored individual is clueless and mildly resentful, involved in a halfhearted, despondent search for something to do that will make a difference.

Clearly, we should speak not of boredom, but of the boredoms, because the notion itself includes a multiplicity of moods and feelings that resist analysis; and this, we can say, is integral to the function of boredom as a kind of blank condensation of psychic life. In that more ordinary, more fleeting, boredom of the child the waiting is repressed. The more common risk for the adult—less attended to, more set in his ways, than the child—is that the boredom will turn into waiting. That the individual will become "brave enough to let his feelings develop" in the absence of an object—toward a possible object, as it were—and by doing so commit himself, or rather, entrust himself, to the inevitable elusiveness of that object. For the adult, it seems, boredom needs to be the more permanent suspended animation of desire. Adulthood, one could say, is when it begins to occur to you that you may not be leading a charmed life.

- 8 -

Looking at Obstacles

The way to solve the problem you see in life is to live
in a way that makes the problem disappear.

Ludwig Wittgenstein, *Culture and Value*

A twelve-year-old girl was referred to me for what turned out
to be an array of symptoms that she had managed to organize
into a school phobia. At the age of ten, having nursed a sense
of neglect in the family, which she perceived as two groups,
the parents and "the girls," her two elder sisters, both leaving
her out, she asked her parents if she could go to boarding school.
This had been an unconscious test of their devotion to her; she
was dismayed to find herself, within three months of the
request, in a public school three hundred miles from home. At
first timid and pliable—the headmistress referred to her as
"sweet and helpful"—she suddenly came to life after a year in
a phobia with which she was terrorizing herself. She was unable
to walk into the classroom; as she said, it made her feel "too
excited," and she thought she would faint or "screech like an
owl." When I said to her in our first awkward meeting that
owls kill at night she thought for a moment and then said with
some relish, "In the dark things don't get in the way." I was
reassured by this because it made me feel that, despite all the
uncertainties and refusals in which she hoarded her rage, she
knew about the fluency in herself. I thought that she no longer
wanted to guard her grudges.

Unusually for a phobic child, she entered into the spirit of
psychotherapy with some vigor after a few months' stubborn
impatience in which, quite sensibly, she treated me as part of
the problem. The only thing that struck me as genuinely odd
about her was her attitude to my holiday breaks. When I told

her of the dates of my holidays or made comments to prepare
her, she treated all these remarks as a kind of hiatus in the
conversation; I felt quite suddenly as though I was talking in
her sleep. She was oblivious but in no way puzzled. Very
politely she would let me have my say, as though I was someone
with an intrusive obsession who every so often needed to blurt
something out about the difficulties of separation. If I got irri-
tated and asked her if she had heard what I was saying, she was
mildly bemused, but it made no difference. She would treat the
sessions before the holiday as quite ordinary and would carry
on the next session as though nothing had come between us. I
found her absolute refusal to take me seriously as someone who
went away rather endearing. I was aware that she had intrigued
me with this, which, in another context, or in someone else,
might have given me serious cause for concern.

And then in the session before the third holiday break she
arrived with an atlas. I had told her, and had been telling her
for some time, that I was going away for two weeks to America.
In what sense she had heard this I had no way of knowing. But
in this session she went straight to the table and traced maps of
America and Britain. She then reproduced them on a piece of
paper and said to me, "While you're *there* [pointing to America],
I'll be *here* [pointing to Britain] making the tea." I said, "That's
amazing! *T* is the difference between here and there"; and she
grinned and said, "So I'll be making the difference." A lot can
be made of this, but for my purposes here I would say that she
could allow herself to recognize the holiday as an obstacle only
when, in fantasy, she could bring it within the range of her own
omnipotence: when she was making the tea. The initial "difference" has to be made, or rather imagined to have been made,
by the subject, not by the object. So the first question is: What
are the preconditions for the recognition of an obstacle? And
the first assertion is: one can recognize an obstacle—which can
mean construct something as an obstacle—only when it can
be tolerated. Only through knowing what we think of as
an obstacle can we understand our fantasies of continuity.

———

In an interview with a couple and their first child, who was now a toddler, the mother was describing how frantic her son made her by his clinging. She couldn't go to the toilet, or go shopping, or do anything without his hanging on to her, wound round her legs. Her description evoked in me the image of somebody running who was gradually being metamorphosed into a tree. She could "never," she said, "have a moment to herself"; he was always—this son who was insinuating himself up and down her body like roots—"in the way." And it was this familiar phrase—"He is always in the way"—that was insistently repeated. It was not difficult to make some sense of all this in terms of the changed relationship between the couple. And it is, of course, put as schematically as this, a common family scenario with children at this developmental stage. But toward the end of the session the thought came into my mind, "Where would she be going if her son was not in the way?" So I asked her, and she replied quite cheerfully, "Oh, I wouldn't know where I was!" The second question then is: How are obstacles unconsciously constructed? And the second assertion is: The obstacle is used to conceal—to pack up, as it were—the unconscious desire. If the child is always in the way—and parents and children may cooperate to ensure that this is the case—then the mother can never find out where she would be going if no one was in the way (of course, one should not underestimate a person's wish to be an obstacle). So one way of describing the family situation is that the mother, or the father, needs the child to cling in order to paralyze any realization—or recognition—of alternative unconscious projects. The obstacle is a way of not letting something else happen, a necessary blind spot.

In *Being and Nothingness* Sartre describes the situation of a walker confronted with an overhanging cliff face. "For the simple traveller," he writes, "who passes over this road and whose free project is a pure aesthetic ordering of the landscape, the crag is not revealed either as scalable or not scalable; it is manifested only as beautiful or ugly."[1] If I am simply on a walk, the rock face is an obstacle; if I am a painter, it is not. But the absurd—the psychoanalytic—possibility that Sartre does not consider is that I may realize I am on a walk only when I perceive the cliff as an obstacle. That is to say, the only way to discover your projects is to notice—to make conscious—what you reckon are obstacles. So the third question would be: What kind of obstacles does one find oneself making, what is one's vocabulary of impediments? (And in clinical terms one could ask: What is the patient's—and, of course, the analyst's—personal repertoire of obstacles?) And the third assertion would be: The desire does not reveal the obstacle; the obstacle reveals the desire. And if only it was as simple as this we could say to our patients, or to ourselves, "Tell me what your obstacles are, and I will tell you what you desire."

There is an apocryphal story about Adler who in his early, more psychoanalytic days, would ask the patient at the end of the first consultation, "What would you do if you were cured?" The patient would answer, and then Adler would say, "Well, go and do it then!"

A thirty-two-year-old man came to see me for a consultation, but very unsure whether his "problem," as he referred to it ironically, warranted psychotherapy, or even consideration as a problem. He talked about how the problem might not be one, but without telling me for some time what it was. He was both jaunty and shy about it all and eventually told me—having made himself rather unavailable—that the problem was that he always fell for "unavailable women." I asked him in what sense they were unavailable, and he said that they always had partners. I said, "Yes, so in what sense are they unavailable?" He smiled and said, "So you mean, what's the problem?" I apologized for being harsh, though in retrospect I think I was also speaking the voice of his disowned rivalry—in psychoanalysis one exaggerates the patient's muted voices—and I replied that he might feel safer with the conviction that they were unavailable, and that we might be able to understand why he needed an obstacle to free his desire. He agreed that he found it slightly reassuring that these women he wanted had men who would protect them from him. I wondered if perhaps he wanted to be protected by a stronger man. And he replied, almost as though it was a proverb, or a piece of folklore, "If you want to get a man, try to get a woman."

It is impossible to imagine desire without obstacles, and wherever we find something to be an obstacle we are at the same time desiring. It is part of the fascination of the Oedipus story in particular, and perhaps of narrative in general, that we and the heroes and heroines of their fictions never know whether obstacles create desire, or desire creates obstacles. We are never quite sure which it is we are seeking, and it is difficult to imagine how to keep the story going without both. So the next question is: Why do we need to think of them as inextricable? And the answer to this question would tell us something interesting about our fictions about desire. A psychoanalytic answer—or rather, response—might be: Desire without obstacles is merging or incest, and so the death of desire; and obstacles without desire are literally unthinkable, or surreal like Magritte's doors suspended in the air.

This apparently inevitable twinning of obstacle and desire suggests, in the case of my male patient, another assertion: The object of unconscious desire can be represented only by the obstacles to the conscious object of desire. This man was conscious of his desire for women, and conscious of their partners as obstacles. But for him the unconscious object of desire was the obstacle, the man. The desire for the object can be used to mask the desire for the obstacle. When we unpack the obstacles in analysis—when we think of them as the way rather than as something in the way—we find them, like Pandora's box, full of the unusual and the forbidden. If I know what I want by coming up against what prevents me from having it, then there must anyway be a wish for obstacles as unconscious mnemonics of desire. The obstacle reminds me of what I want, in one part of my mind, to forget.

Symptoms, of course, are always construed by the patient as obstacles; so it is always worth wondering what the patient's imaginary unobstructed life would look like in the absence of such constraints. What are the catastrophic—or catastrophically pleasurable—scenarios that his cherished obstacles both protect him from and sustain as an anticipated possibility in an always deferred future? "Countless times," Rousseau writes in book 1 of the *Confessions,*

> during my apprenticeship and since, I have gone out with the idea of buying some sweet thing. As I come to the pastry cook's I catch sight of the women behind the counter and can already imagine them laughing among themselves and making fun of the greedy youngster. Then I pass a fruiterer's and look at the ripe pears out of the corner of my eye; the scent of them tempts me. But two or three young people over there are looking at me; a man I know is standing in front of the shop; I can see a girl coming in the distance. Is she not our maidservant? My short sight is constantly deceiving me. I take everyone who passes for someone I know. I am frightened by everything and discover obstacles everywhere. As my discomfort grows my desire increases. But in the end I go home like an idiot, consumed by longing and with money enough in my pocket to satisfy it, but not having dared to buy anything.[2]

Satisfaction for Rousseau is the death of possibility. So Rousseau needs not to master the obstacles, but to nurture them. Anticipation is the mother of invention. And in his commitment to innocence there is always the covert suggestion that nothing is forbidden, that we are not controlling ourselves, just finding ways of making what we don't do more exciting. In this almost frenzied and certainly fraught scenario we find Rousseau's wish to make a spectacle of his desire apparently controlled by the projected disapproval of others. He creates an entirely reassuring and familiar world—"I take everyone who passes for someone I know"—policed by exciting obstacles. And this catalogue of obstacles—the women behind the counter, the young people, the man, and the maid—he supposes to be excessively interested in his desire. He has money in his pocket, but he needs these obstacles to make his ordinary desire seem, at least to himself, criminal. If it is dangerous to buy a ripe pear, only a dangerous man can do it. If his aliveness or his potency is in doubt — and how could they not be?—then the obstacles he creates have the effect of making his desire seem inordinately powerful; so powerful in fact, so socially disruptive, that the audience he has simulated forgets everything else. He is unable to think what would happen if no one was at all interested in his desire. "I am frightened by everything," he writes, "and discover obstacles everywhere." But he is frightened by everything—that is, excited by everything—*because* he discovers obstacles everywhere; because every obstacle makes him potentially a criminal. And if Rousseau is not unconsciously a criminal he is not, in his own eyes at least, a man.

What Rousseau alerts us to here is the passion for obstacles. And this leads me to the next assertion: The first relationship is not with objects but with obstacles. Or to put it another way, from the other end, so to speak: People fall in love at the moments in their lives when they are most terrorized by possibilities. In order to fall in love with someone they must be perceived to be an obstacle, a necessary obstacle.

"We can only laugh," Freud wrote, "when a joke has come to our help." It is as though we need something to release, or permit, the laugh that is already inside us. It is through the joke, Freud suggests, that we are momentarily released from the obstacles we have imposed on our pleasure. It is, in fact, in *Jokes and Their Relation to the Unconscious* that Freud uses the word *obstacle*—at least in the English translation—with the greatest frequency. And the joke is so important for Freud because it is the most ingeniously efficient way of rescuing our pleasure from the obstacles. And rescuing pleasure, in Freud's terms, is a form of remembrance. Jokes

> make possible the satisfaction of an instinct (whether lustful or hostile) in the face of an obstacle that stands in its way. They circumvent this obstacle and in that way draw pleasure from a source which the obstacle had made inaccessible . . . The repressive activity of civilisation brings

it about that primary possibilities of enjoyment, which
have now, however, been repudiated by the censorship
in us, are lost to us. But to the human psyche all renunciation is exceedingly difficult, and so we find that tendentious jokes provide a means of undoing the renunciation and retrieving what was lost.[3]

Jokes, like dreams, are the saboteurs of repression. Civilization
makes an obstacle course of our pleasures, but jokes link us to
our losses, what Freud calls our "primary possibilities of enjoyment." The obstacles keep us safe, but the joke endangers us
with excitement. What Freud makes less explicit is that the
obstacle provides us with an additional source of pleasure—the
pleasure to be got from successfully circumventing the obstacle.
Outwitting is the other soul of wit. So there is always an ironic
sense in which the search for obstacles is also the search for
pleasure. ("Failure to understand a joke," as Proust's narrator
reminds us, "has never yet made anyone find it less amusing.")[4]
One of the aims of psychoanalytic treatment may be to enable
the patient to find, or be able to tolerate, more satisfying obstacles to contend with. Poor obstacles impoverish us.

———

An obstacle is literally something that stands in the way,
a "hindrance, impediment, obstruction . . . resistance, objec-
tion" as the Oxford English Dictionary has it, adding a seventeenth-century usage of "to make obstacle," meaning "to offer
opposition." These definitions are all obviously suggestive in
relation to psychoanalytic theory. In the repetition compulsion,
for example, what is the obstacle, what prevents the patient
from organizing a more exact repetition? Or to think of resistance as the construction of an obstacle might lead us to redescribe resistances as peculiarly inventive artifacts. "The real
resistance," Sandor Ferenczi and Otto Rank write in The Development of Psycho-Analysis, "far from disturbing the analytic
work is actually a requisite and acts as a mainspring in regulating
its course . . . the content of the resistance is also of importance
for it almost always is a sign that the patient here too repro-
duces instead of remembers and in the material betrays also that

which he would like by means of reproduction to withdraw from analytic elaboration."[5] The resistance encodes the past that, by being repeated rather than remembered, is an obstacle to the future. Like all defenses it apparently forecloses the future, one thing the patient and the analyst will never know anything about. What is repressed in advance is the novelty of experience. The obstacle of repetition—resistance as repetition—creates the illusion of foresight. And psychoanalytic theory can collude with this by implying that the future is merely the past in different terms.

As George Crabbe writes in his once extremely popular *English Synonymes Explained* (1818), "the obstacle opposes itself, it is properly met in the way, and intervenes between us and our object." And just in case we might forget that, from a psychoanalytic point of view, the fetish, after the father, is the paradigmatic obstacle, Crabbe gives us as a further definition: "in latin *obstaculum* from *obsta* to stand in the way, signifies the thing that stands in the way between the person and the object that he has in view." Given the emphasis on the visual here—the object in view—it is always worth considering which of the senses is being used for analogy in the construction of the obstacle. I can smell and hear round corners; if there is a wall between us I won't be able to taste you.

"The thing that stands in the way between the person and the object he has in view" is Freud's description of the making of a fetish. "When the fetish is instituted . . . the subject's interest comes to a halt half-way, as it were; it is as though the last impression before the uncanny and traumatic one is retained as a fetish. Thus the foot or shoe owes its preference as a fetish— or part of it—to the circumstances that the inquisitive boy peered at the women's genital from below, from her legs up."[6] The terror of castration, Freud claims, and thus the loss of bodily integrity, produces a need to find obstacles to the perception that there are two sexes. The fetish sponsors the idea that there is nothing to lose. As Victor Smirnoff says, the fetishist is "someone who is trying to secure a triple guarantee— to make good his fundamental loss, to maintain and assure continuity, and to recognize his own sexual status in relation to the fantasy of the phallic mother."[7] But the irony of this obstacle, the fetish, is that it is needed to stop the fetishist from seeing what he has already seen, what Smirnoff calls, "his fundamental loss." Like all defenses it is a form of acknowledgment, a tolerable way of thinking about something unacceptable. What the boy first saw, in fantasy, as it were, was that there was no obstacle—or was the penis an obstacle?—to becoming a woman. What was absent was an obstacle to castration.

"The fetish," Freud writes, "is a substitute for the mother's penis," so it provides an obstacle to the thought "A person can lose a penis," and an obstacle to the thought "I'm different from my mother." "He has retained the belief [that a woman has a penis]," Freud writes, "but he has also given it up."[8] Just as it is the sign of a good theory that it can be used to support contradictory positions, it is the sign of a good fetish that it keeps incompatible ideas alive. The obstacle that is found to seeing the female genitals—a shoe in Freud's example—is a way of sustaining belief that there are two sexes and denying it at the same time. The obstacle secretly confronts the fetishist with what it protects him from. But the object of desire is unbearable without the obstacle of the fetish.

But how can one have, as Freud suggests, and indeed keeps recurring to throughout his work, opposing "currents" in mental life? In the essay on fetishism he describes two boys for whom "it was only one current in their mental life that had not recognised their father's death; there was another current that took full account of that fact."[9] How can we describe the obstacles—which are fantasies—that stop these contradictory thoughts from contaminating each other? Perhaps we talk too much about dissociation without trying to describe what we put between states of mind to keep them apart. And this is a particularly interesting project because what keeps them apart—and this is the essence of the obstacle—also links them. Sometimes, in fact, what keeps things apart may be the only connection between them. In the attack on linking, the attack becomes the link.

Once we are talking of this paradox of the link that separates we are inevitably reminded of Winnicott's apparently
familiar concept of the transitional object, something that comes
between to make a more facilitating connection. The inter-
mediate area of transitional phenomena, he writes, "exists as a
resting place for the individual engaged in the perpetual human
task of keeping inner and outer reality separate yet interrelated."
It is with the idea of transitional phenomena that Winnicott
introduces something that I think should be called obstacle-rela-
tions as an addition, or perhaps an alternative, to object-relations. If the fetish is an acknowledgment through disavowal of
the threat of castration, the transitional object is an acknowledgment through mediation of the dual threat of merging and absolute isolation. And this dual threat we think of as pre-oedipal
in origin. We could, in fact, describe the differences between
the oedipal and the pre-oedipal in terms of the difference of
obstacles. Winnicott, however, never makes clear the connection between the use of transitional objects and the shift from
pre-oedipal to oedipal relationships. He writes only that "the
object represents the infant's transition from the state of being
in relation to the mother as something outside and separate."
It is an obstacle to merging and absolute loss—the two fundamental terrors construed by psychoanalysis—and so creates the
space for experiencing. In the transitional space neither threat
is preemptive or overwhelming. "The term transitional object,"
he writes, "according to my suggestion, gives room for the
process of becoming able to accept difference and similarity,"[10]
unlike the fetish, one might add, which out of the terror of
difference is used to simulate sameness. In this "process of
becoming able to accept difference and similarity," difference
entails the making or finding of obstacles, similarity the relin-
quishing or destroying of obstacles.

There are no obstacles to one's own death, but the obstacles
to murder are unsurprising. The second murderer in *Richard III*,
describing conscience, says to his accomplice: "'Tis a blushing,
shamefac'd spirit that mutinies in a man's bosom. It fills a man
full of obstacles." It is to the filling and emptying of obstacles

in a person's life—at its most extreme in manic-depressive states—that we should turn our attention if we wish to understand something new about the conundrum of sameness and difference. The obstacle makes the difference; so in developmental terms it is the obstacle that makes possible the object, that makes possible the idea of someone else.

A person's life, we should remember, in the terms of Freud's later work, was described as an obstacle between two quiescent states. But then Freud believed in the opposition, the antagonism, between life and death.

I was standing one day in a line in a post office in Camberwell, and a small child in a stroller in the line next to me kept throwing her doll away, much to her mother's annoyance. Each time it happened the mother retrieved it, much to the child's surprise, and then it was immediately thrown away again. After about the fifth or sixth time the mother brought the doll back and said crossly to her daughter, "If you lose that you've had it." This struck me then as rather an interesting remark. Obviously I have no idea what the child made of it—although she did stop throwing out the doll—and I have some idea of what the mother intended. But it did occur to me that this little girl may have been trying to find out something about what came between herself and an object—what the distance or the difference was made of—and how it is removed. To throw away the doll was to impose an obstacle, and by doing so to find out something about the object. This is the kind of object that only certain obstacles can come between; and these certain obstacles seem, at least at first, to be automatically removed by the mother. If she had finally lost it—found an absolute obstacle to its presence—she would indeed have had it in a specific sense.

In a commentary on Simone Weil's statement that "All human progress consists in changing constraint into an obstacle," the philosopher Peter Winch writes: "When I see things as obstacles I am already on the way to investigating and developing systematic ideas about their properties and interrelations; about the necessities to which they are subject." What I am suggesting is that the child can find out what the object is—or rather, get a version of what it might be, its properties and interrelations—only by finding or constructing obstacles to its access or availability. The search for obstacles—the need to impose them in their familiar guise of time and space—is part of the endless, baffled inquiry into the nature of the object. I know what something or someone is by finding out what comes between us.

The little girl throwing her doll away is, of course, reminiscent of Freud's description of his grandson's Fort-Da game. When the child discovers the cotton-reel, that he can pull back what he has thrown away, Freud suggests, he is on his way to mastering, by symbolic substitution, the absence imposed upon him by his mother. The child is beginning to work out what it is that is between people, which is related to what it is that comes between people. There is no thread of cotton connecting them; rather, he is hanging by the thread of his wishful desire. But the existence of that extraordinary phenomena, the wish, always implies a prior perception of obstacles. After all, why would we need to wish if nothing were in the way?

The way we get to know what we eventually call a mother is through the obstacles to her presence. To feel hunger is to feel a growing obstacle to its gratification. In what Winnicott calls the "moment of illusion"—the moment of desire when it is imagined that the infant fantasizes the edible mother and she actually feeds him—it is as though the object of desire emerges out of the obstacles to her presence, as out of a fog. At the beginning, perhaps, there is not a mother in mind, but an obstacle to a mother; not a mother that is absent, but an obstacle that is present. (Another way of saying this would be to ask the slightly absurd question, Is the first thought the absence of mother or the presence of time?) At the so-called beginning the child enters not a world of objects, but a world of obstacles. Consciousness is of obstacles. Wherever you look, as the Chinese proverb says, there's something in the way.

The unconscious in Freud's description is, so to speak, a place without obstacles; or rather, a world immune from the obstacles created by what he calls secondary process thinking; a world, he writes, "exempt from mutual contradiction . . . There are in this system, no negation, no doubt, no degrees of certainty"; the unconscious, he mentions on several occasions, is "timeless."[12] So a good question to ask of a dream—indeed a question often crucial to its interpretation—is, What are the obstacles that have been removed to make this extraordinary scene possible? In the Freudian topography we are not only, in the familiar formula, half man half beast; we are also composed of two worlds: a world without the usual obstacles—the unconscious that Freud called "the other place"—and a world that is an obstacle-course, a world presided over by the ego in its desperate search for obstacles. And interpretation—the linking of these two worlds—becomes nothing more than the addition, subtraction, or modification of obstacles.

John Cage said in an interview that it was through reading D. T. Suzuki on Zen Buddhism that he came to realize that "sound no longer comprises an obstacle to silence; silence is no longer a screen with regard to sound."[13] Perhaps this is one way of picturing something as really bizarre, something as virtually unthinkable, as the Freudian unconscious. The unconscious as a "seething cauldron" is easier to imagine than a place without obstacles. And without obstacles the notion of development, at least in its progressivist sense, is inconceivable. There would be nothing to master.

I wrote this essay to show that obstacles are the clue to desire, that the word is full of meaning. But I have an uneasy feeling, which we probably all remember from childhood, and which may be pertinent to the subject at hand; the feeling that comes when one endlessly repeats a word only to be left with an enigmatic obstacle as to its sense.

- 9 -

Plotting for Kisses

These violent delights have violent ends,
And in their triumph die like fire and powder,
Which as they kiss consume.

Friar Laurence in *Romeo and Juliet*

An eight-year-old girl tells me in a session how much she loves being in the countryside on holiday. I ask what she likes doing there, and she replies, with a kind of blithe indifference, "Oh, sometimes I just go out looking . . . for cows, birds, kisses, things like that." "Kisses?" I ask. "You know, lovers . . . I hate it when people kiss, their mouths get muddled up."

A boy of seventeen who has been trying for weeks to work out what it is about his girlfriend that is "driving him mad"— the frustration, that is to say, for which he uses her—arrives at his session in an unusually bumptious mood. He has realized, he announces to me triumphantly, what it is about her: "She doesn't kiss properly." He mooches around in his mind for more to say, but to his own surprise he is blank, so I offer him a suggestion: "When people kiss they've stopped talking. If her kisses were words, what would they be saying to you?" "You can't really love someone that you don't love kissing," he replies, as though oblivious to my question.

In 1930 Sandor Ferenczi, speculating along what were by then traditional psychoanalytic lines about what he called "oral eroticism in education," wrote in his journal: "It is not impossible that the question of how much oral eroticism (sucking the breasts, the thumb, the dummy—kissing) should be allowed or even offered to the suckling, and later in the period of weaning, is of paramount importance for the development of character."[1] In his repertoire of the infant's oral eroticism kissing, placed at the end of the list, is the anomalous element. It includes sucking, of course, but this is not its definitive characteristic. With the mouth's extraordinary virtuosity, it involves some of the pleasures of eating in the absence of nourishment. But of all self-comforting or autoerotic activities the most ludicrous, the most obviously unsatisfying and therefore infrequent, is kissing oneself.

In the same entry Ferenczi goes on to reconstruct the trauma that certain oral activities try to undo:

> Obviously the love life of the newly born begins as complete passivity. Withdrawal of love leads to undeniable feelings of being deserted. The consequence is the splitting of the personality into two halves, one of which plays the role of the mother (thumb sucking: thumb is equalled with mother's breast). Prior to the splitting there is probably a tendency to self-destruction caused by the trauma, which tendency, however, can still be inhibited—so to speak—on its way: out of the chaos a new kind of order is created which is then adapted to the precarious external circumstances.

Ferenczi imagines the terror—the invisible history—out of which such banal, self-comforting behavior as thumb sucking may arise. He assumes that the infant must in a sense choose in this primal crisis between self-destruction or a new kind of relationship with himself by taking flight to his own body. Bereft and relatively powerless, in a precocious, desperate attempt to become for the time being his own mother, the infant splits his personality and sucks his thumb. His body then becomes, in a familiar cliché, the first mother-substitute. The child will develop more-sophisticated ways of dealing with his own insufficiency, but there is one thing he will not do, one thing it is as though, Freud suggests, he will defer until adolescence. The child may stroke or suck himself, or kiss other people and things, but he will not kiss himself. Eventually, Freud writes in the *Three Essays on the Theory of Sexuality*, he will kiss other people on the mouth because he is unable to kiss himself there. Kissing, as we shall see—and it is hardly surprising in retrospect—is central in an oblique way to Freud's theory of sexual development. One way out of the chaos Ferenczi describes, part of the new order, is the belated desire to kiss another person on the mouth.

Adults tend to have strong, mostly private and embarrassed feelings about kissing. But this squeamishness—it would be silly or arch to be interested in kisses—conceals an intense, originally infantile curiosity about kissing and a repertoire of different kinds of kisses. It is, for example, one of the commonest infantile sexual theories that babies are conceived by kissing; like most infantile sexual theories, this is anatomically inaccurate but suggestive and metonymically correct. Children are right by implication about kissing. And as Freud recognized, these infantile sexual theories are not relinquished after children are told the so-called facts of life. "After such enlightenment," he writes,

> children know something that they did not know before, but they make no use of the new knowledge that has been presented to them . . . They behave like primitive races who have had Christianity thrust upon them and who continue to worship their old idols in secret.[2]

It is worth wondering, perhaps, what the wishes are in kissing.

At certain periods of our lives we spend a lot of time plotting for kisses, not only as foreplay but also as ends in themselves. It is of course considered adolescent—and by adolescent boys effeminate—to be a connoisseur of such things, although adolescence too easily involves, as only adults can know, the putting away of the wrong childish things. Ostentatious kisses are usually represented in the most popular and once intellectually disparaged genres, romantic novels and films. And although there are clearly conventions in literature and life governing the giving and getting of kisses, it is really only from films that we can learn what the contemporary conventions might be for kissing itself. Styles of kissing can be seen but not easily described, as though kissing resists verbal representation. It is striking that, unlike other forms of sexuality, there is little synonymy of kissing. It has generated no familiar slang, acquired virtually no language in which it can be redescribed. It is not merely that in the romance of appetite the details of salivation are not compelling. Apparently for the sake of interest stories often ignore, in a way films do not, the fact that the kiss itself is a story in miniature, a subplot.

From a psychoanalytic point of view, the kiss is a revealing sequence containing a personal history. The way a person kisses and likes to be kissed shows in condensed form something about that person's character. In what Freud saw as the individual's biphasic sexual development, kissing, as a relatively late version of oral eroticism, links us to our earliest relationship with ourselves and other people. It is integral to the individual's ongoing project of working out what mouths are for. In that craving for other mouths that is central to the experience of adolescence and seems to begin then, the individual resumes with newfound intensity of appetite and inhibition his oral education, connected now with an emerging capacity for genital sexuality. There is the return of the primary sensuous experience of tasting another person, one in which the difference between the sexes can supposedly be attenuated—the kiss is the image of reciprocity, not of domination—but one that is also unprecedented developmentally, since it includes tasting someone else's mouth. Although this is prefigured in the childhood game of touching tongues, children are usually appalled at the idea of putting their tongues in each other's mouths; partly because kissing signifies an inhibited rehearsal for intercourse and other sexual practices, with all the attendant anxieties. Through kissing the erotics of greed contend again, as in childhood, with the reassurances of concern; and again, directly in relation to another person's body. "Animals can be tamed," Winnicott wrote ominously, "but not mouths."[3] Kissing, though, is the sign of taming, of controlling the potential—at least in fantasy—to bite up and ingest the other person. Lips, as it were, are the next thing to teeth, and teeth are great educators.

Mouths learn to kiss. So in psychoanalytic terms kissing may be, among other things, a compromise solution to what Freud saw as the individual's primary ambivalence, and a way of gratifying that other appetite he recognized: the appetite for pleasure independent of the desire for nourishment or reproduction. When we kiss we devour the object by caressing it; we eat it, in a sense, but sustain its presence. Kissing on the mouth can have a mutuality that blurs the distinctions between giving and taking ("In kissing do you render or receive?" Cressida asks in *Troilus and Cressida*). If in a crude psychoanalytic interpretation kissing could be described as aim-inhibited eating, we should also consider the more nonsensical option that eating can also be, as Freud will imply, aim-inhibited kissing.

In the *Three Essays on the Theory of Sexuality* Freud emphasizes the significance of the fact that the individual's first and most formative relationship to the world is an oral one, that "sucking at his mother's breast has become the prototype of every relation of love." He describes kissing in his master-plot of development as what might be called a normal perversion, an ordinary sexual activity that is perverse only in the psychoanalytic sense that it can be used as, or become, a substitute for genital intercourse (it is of interest that there are no common sexual perversions involving kissing as opposed to licking, sucking, or eating). "Even a kiss," Freud writes,

> can claim to be described as a perverse act, since it consists in the bringing together of two oral erotogenic zones instead of two genitals. Yet no one rejects it as perverse; on the contrary it is permitted in theatrical performances as a softened hint at the sexual act.[4]

The kiss, blurring the boundary between the normal and the perverse, is—perhaps for that same reason—the publicly acceptable representation of private sexual life, a performed allusion to it. Revealing like no other oral activity the powerful connection, in fantasy and physiology, between mouths and genitals, kissing is indeed a "softened hint" at the sexual act. When Bob Dylan sings of a kiss, "her mouth was watery and wet,"[5] he is referring to the fact that not everything that is wet is watery.

In a well-known paragraph from the *Three Essays,* one that probably lingered at the back of Ferenczi's mind, Freud makes more ambitious claims for the possible significance of kissing. "To begin with," he writes of the infant, "sexual activity attaches itself to functions serving the purpose of self-preservation and does not become independent of them till later." A time comes for the infant when the sensual pleasure of sucking the breast is unaccompanied by the need for nourishment and can be split off from it. Through his mouth the infant experiences a division of claims, a new quality of life. Two parallel orders of desire develop that can overlap but do not need to: one more evidently purposive and bound up with the need for nourishment; the other less easy to describe but referred to by Freud as sexual, having to do with the pleasure of pleasure:

> The need for repeating the sexual satisfaction now becomes detached from the need for taking nourishment—a separation which becomes inevitable when the teeth appear and food is no longer taken in only by sucking but is also chewed up. The child does not make use of an extraneous body for his sucking but prefers a part of his own skin because it is more convenient, because it makes him independent of the external world, which he is not yet able to control, and because in that way he provides himself, as it were, with a second erotogenic zone, though one of an inferior kind. The inferiority of this second region is among the reasons why, at a later date, he seeks the corresponding part—the lips—of another person. ("It's a pity I can't kiss myself," he seems to be saying.)[6]

The separation becomes "inevitable," Freud surmises, when the possibility of real destructiveness enters the picture. (In 1838 Darwin had noted in his journal "one's tendency to kiss, & almost bite, that which one sexually loves.") Of necessity the infant turns to the object for nourishment but away from the object for what Freud advertently calls "sexual satisfaction." He cannot eat himself, although he can pleasure himself by sucking parts of his own body. But this second erotogenic zone, his own skin, is inferior to the mother's breast as a source of pleasure. It is worth noting that Freud does not say here that it is inferior because it is inedible or because it is more available; he simply states by way of conclusion that it just is less satisfying. And it is not, in his account, the breasts or the genitals of another person that are then immediately sought out at "a later date" but another mouth, and then not only to suck. Because the mouth, unlike the body parts it sucks, is acutely alive to its own pleasure, it therefore seeks, Freud seems to be suggesting, by that same narcissistic logic, its curious reunion through another person's lips.

It is perhaps useful to summarize the extraordinary sequence Freud proposes for the individual's primary object of being at least sexually self-satisfied, given that he cannot initially feed himself; the journey, that is to say, from sucking to kissing. At first pleasure and nourishment are inextricable; then the infant experiences a new pleasure that Freud calls sexual satisfaction, which is independent of nourishment but still dependent on the object. The infant then substitutes his own body as the object of this separate pleasure and later seeks, among other things, the "corresponding part" of another person's body: the mouth, the only part of his body he can never kiss in the mirror. Finally Freud offers by implication the intriguing, grotesque—almost unthinkable—image of a person kissing his own mouth, and suggests that it is a narcissistic blow that he is unable to do so.

This eventual kiss highlights for Freud a double disappointment that is integral to his conception of human development: disappointment with the object because its independence makes it, as it were, the primal inconvenience; disappointment with the self because it cannot be the original or the sufficiently gratifying object. The individual's first and forever-recurring loss, in Freud's view, is not of the object but of the fantasy of self-sufficiency, of being everything to oneself. In adolescence the individual will substitute, Freud says, the "inferiority" of his own skin for the further disillusionment that is at the same time an intensely evocative pleasure, of kissing another person's mouth. But why does Freud draw a conclusion so unexpected, so remote from the ordinary experiences of kissing and being kissed?

For Freud, development was a process of substitution in which there were no substitutes, merely necessary alternatives. Given the hopelessness of the individual's attempts to be sexually self-satisfied—represented here as the impossibility of kissing one's own mouth—Freud, I think, saw kissing as confirming his sense of the narcissistic intent, the grudge at the root of sexuality: a grudge, that is to say, contingent upon the cumulative trauma that is human development. Desire, he wants us to know, is always in excess of the object's capacity to satisfy it. The object of desire, like the kiss that is by definition a mistake in Chekhov's story "The Kiss," is resonant, finally, because it disappoints; and because it disappoints it can be returned to. Harmless, the kiss is a symbol of betrayal, and of the revisions that betrayal always brings in its wake.

What, then, to ask the simple psychoanalytic question, are the fantasies in kissing? We usually smile beforehand, and often close our eyes. We kiss our children goodnight, although it is not immediately obvious why we do so; and we are, of course, unsurprised that traditionally prostitutes never kiss their clients on the mouth. Kisses—of which it can be said, despite our misgivings, that there are many kinds and that they have always punctuated our lives—are a threat and a promise, the signature as cliché of the erotic. And therefore, as Freud knew, they involve us in the dangerous allure and confusion of mistaken identity, of getting muddled up. In *The Anatomy of Melancholy* Burton writes: "To kiss and be kissed, . . . amongst other things, is as a burden in a song, and a most forcible battery, as infectious, Xenophon thinks, as the poison of a spider."[7] Truly infectious, kissing may be our most furtive, our most reticent sexual act, the mouth's elegy to itself.

- 10 -

Playing Mothers: Between Pedagogy and Transference

> If there's nowhere to rest at the end
> how can I get lost on the way?
>
> Ikkyu, *Crow with No Mouth*

Free-floating attention, the notoriously anonymous mirror, the telephone of unconscious communication: as targets for identification, as instructions in how to behave as a psychoanalyst, they are not prescriptive with regard to sex. Of course, Freud's minimalism here and everywhere else in his writing about technique, invites interpretation—What *does* one use a mirror for? Can one *teach* people to float, in their minds?— but these analogies are strikingly neuter. By virtue of practicing as an analyst a person does not thereby turn himself into one sex or another; that is what the patient is supposed to do to him.

The transference is always something the analyst didn't know he was expecting until it arrives. It is integral to the psychoanalytic process that the analyst cannot know beforehand which sex he is going to be. The analyst is always waiting for the patient to tell him—and then to discover what the assumed, the unconscious consequences are of such an invitation. The psychoanalytic setting is a frame for unanticipated invitations. And these attributions of apparent sexual identity bring with them a largely unconscious repertoire of permissions and pro-hibitions to act, of wished-up assumptions of sexual entitle-ment. Each sex is categorized according to unconscious fantasies of function, which are always fantasies of possible drama. The analyst is not only the one who is supposed to know, but also the one who is expected to act: as someone in particular, as

someone special, but as someone on the move. So-called analytic neutrality is a paradoxical estrangement technique, devised
to evoke a familiarization. The analyst is the perfect stranger
usable in words.

But transference depends upon the possibility of psychic
mobility; by sitting still the analyst becomes a moving target.
What is being prepared, as Freud said, is an unknowable set of
"new editions and facsimiles," reissues with a new introduction.
It is one of the problematic consequences of what became
British object-relations theory—indeed, an irony from which
it does not know how to recover—that despite the inevitable
vagaries of the patient's transference the analyst always knows
fundamentally whom he will be experienced as at the "deepest"
levels of the patient's personality. Although he is not in actuality
the patient's mother—with the notable exception of Klein's
analysis of her own children—he is playing mother if and when
he is analyzing the patient's most "primitive" pre-oedipal con-
flicts. The transference, in other words, is both facilitated and
preempted. Unlike the dream, it can be expected. If the analysis
is done properly it will arrive on time. But there is, of course,
an uneasy fit—a difference that makes all the difference—
between what mothers supposedly do and what analysts are
supposed only to say. If, as Winnicott said, a good interpretation can be like a good feed, then mothering has replaced dreaming as the royal road to the unconscious. One can be given a
good feed but not a good dream. One can be demanding of
dreams, as psychoanalysis is, but one cannot demand a dream.

Mothers, as we shall see, were used by the British School
theorists, as though they were a genus, to provide descriptions
of what psychoanalysts were supposed to be doing. They
became models for a new profession that had uniquely prob-
lematized the question of the model, of the production of
paradigms. After all, from whom, by what process can a person
learn—or rather, become—an analyst? To avert the catastrophe
of the potentially endless charade of identifications—and to preclude addressing the question, What do analysts want?—mothers
were looked at, or rather observed, for the answers. "It has been

to mothers," Winnicott wrote, "that I have so deeply needed to speak."[1] Clearly, the discovery of transference was still not incompatible with the idea that mother had the answers.

Whereas in Freud's writing there are a few cursory descriptions of mothering as the ordinary business of nurture, we find explicitly in the writing of Anna Freud, D. W. Winnicott, Ronald Fairbairn, John Bowlby, Wilfred Bion—and implicitly in Melanie Klein in a way that neither she nor her followers were usually prepared to concede[2]—a precise sense, derived in part from empirical observation, of the mother's function and the pathological consequences of its "failure." Psychoanalysis was being used to reinforce, and not to dispel, the notion of the normative life-story. Mothers were burdened, once again, with all the disappointments of wisdom.

From one point of view—and not only the point of view of an improbable progressivism—Freud's lack of interest in a phenomenology of mothering was a serious omission. But it was an omission that freed him to ask a new kind of question, one particularly pertinent to the psychoanalyst as acolyte: What does my wanting to be like someone—anyone—tell me about my desire?

> He who returns has never left.
>
> Pablo Neruda, "Adioses"

In the work of the British School psychoanalysis was not used as a new way to understand mothering, but mothering was used to understand psychoanalysis. Psychoanalysts began to write as though they could be taught by mothers what to do. The study of mothers and infants, which so quickly became the focus of psychoanalytic research in Britain after the war, became the matrix for the study of psychoanalysis. Here, it was believed, reconstruction could be scientifically informed by observation, by seeing what really happens (empiricism is always in an optative mood). Just as Freud had at first learned so much from seeing Charcot's hysterics perform, now the aspiring analyst could watch the mother and her child perform.

But then, of course, Freud had found that he had learned something quite different just from listening. What was to differentiate psychoanalysis from its precursors was that the dream was considered a better model than the spectacle, the visual object that cannot be seen.

What emerged from this increasingly sophisticated form of observation were canonical fantasies about mothering that became paradigmatic for the otherwise puzzling—because unprecedented—practice of psychoanalysis. The language found for these observations enabled psychoanalysis to rejoin the mainstream of social engineering. Developmental theory—psychoanalysis without the exaggerations, as Adorno might have said—was instrumental reason in what should have been an uncongenial context. The mother, Anna Freud wrote in her influential schema of developmental lines, "becomes not only the child's first (anaclitic, need-fulfilling) object but also the first external legislator. The first external laws with which she confronts the infant are concerned with the *timing* and *rationing* of his satisfaction." [3] Why, one can ask now, did she describe it in these terms? Why was this the vocabulary—the language-game—that came to mind? Because, of course, these were the terms that could be used both to teach the always elusive work of the psychoanalyst and to make psychoanalysis compatible with more-traditional social practices. Legislation, timing, and rationing: to help a person on his way; a vocabulary that constituted the skill of the psychoanalyst simply by describing a mother. It was the psychoanalyst making himself a promise. Was it not, after all, timing and rationing, not to mention legislation, that were the bones of contention that split psychoanalytic groups after Freud?

Freud had made it possible to ask the question, a question that would change the nature of pedagogy and therefore of ethical inquiry, What is there in, or about, the human subject that is both prior to and beyond identification? In British psychoanalysis—from the Controversial Discussions to the current emphasis on infant-observation in analytic training—the more traditional, irrepressible question returned: not, How is one, through the transference, to analyze identifications—and so the nature of identification itself—but How is one to establish identifications on firmer ground?[4] Could transference, in other words, through the observation of mothers and infants, be resolved into pedagogy? Because whenever psychoanalysts speak about development it seems as though they are talking about psychoanalysis as pedagogy, psychoanalysis as the transmission of scientific information about human nature. When the psychoanalyst speaks about development he stops being the one who is supposed to know. Transference, after all, has to stop somewhere . . .

To be a psychoanalyst, then, whom must I be able to identify with, or recognize myself being identified as by the patient? If developmental theory was one attempt to fix, to ground the transference, the more interesting because more paradoxical attempt was derived from Klein's work with what she saw as the most primitive anxieties that defined the human condition. Of course, verbal analysis of preverbal states was likely to create a certain vertigo in the analyst, a fear of heights that could masquerade as a fear of depths. Winnicott's concept of holding and Bion's concept of reverie—the two formative paradigms of analytic technique in the British School—use a version of the pre-oedipal mother as psychoanalytic mentor. As such, they were bids to determine the analyst's function through a gender-specific identification.

> All women become like their mothers. That is their
> tragedy. No man does. That is his.
>
> Oscar Wilde, *The Importance of Being Earnest*

Describing the process of "maternal reverie," Bion writes: "Normal development follows if the relationship between the infant and breast permits the infant to project a feeling, say, that it is dying into the mother and to reintroject it after its sojourn in the breast has made it tolerable to the infant psyche." This is not a hermeneutic of suspicion but—as the biblical word *sojourn* suggests—a process of albeit difficult hospitality. In this alchemy of maternal digestion and recycling the mother and the analyst metabolize the primitive inchoate emotionality of the infant—and the most regressed patient—to produce meaning, what Bion refers to as usable "sense-data." Interpretation becomes visceral; in a rather literal—but no less useful—analogy, body-based. "The mother's capacity for reverie," he writes, in his catastrophic pastoral of normal development, "is the receptor organ for the infant's harvest of self-sensation gained by its conscious."[5] The mother, like the analyst, has to sow what she reaps. To be able, in Bion's sense, to learn from experience in analysis is to be able to tolerate hearing the transference interpreted; and this depends on the analyst's having made it tolerable through what is effectively redescription. One can learn from experience, but one cannot be taught by it.

But is this receptor-organ—referred to by Bion apparently without irony—an acquired characteristic, so to speak? Does the analyst learn how to have it, or learn how to use it? Despite the prevalence of a certain kind of pedagogical analogy in Bion's work—an emphasis on "learning from experience," to use his title, with its teleology of accumulation—this organ is not, in any obvious sense, a "method" of interpretation. It is a state of mind as act of faith; just as for Winnicott—in a paradox that easily becomes a mystification—there can be learning in psychoanalysis, but there must not be teaching. "I never use long sentences," Winnicott writes vis-à-vis interpretation, "unless I am very tired. If I am near exhaustion point I begin teaching." But he interprets because "if I make none the patient gets the impression that I understand everything."[6] To become the teacher is to be seduced by the transference, and so to teach is to seduce. And of course, if one understands everything there is no one to teach. But those—like Bion and Winnicott—who are most impressed by the pre-oedipal mother in psychoanalysis are always poised in their writing between an extreme authoritativeness and an absolute skepticism, between having something to teach, and only being supposed to know; between omniscience and its identical opposite.

"So much depends," Winnicott wrote in a book he did not

live to entitle *Human Nature,* "on the way the mother holds the baby, and let it be emphasised that this is not something that can be taught." And yet holding, as he observed it in mothers, was a virtual definition for Winnicott of the psychoanalytic process; whether it be through the analyst's maintaining the reliability and resilience of the setting, through interpretation, or both. "A correct and well-timed interpretation," he writes in *Human Nature,* "in an analytic treatment gives a sense of being held physically that is more real (to the non-psychotic) than if a real holding or nursing had taken place."[7] There is, in other words, a contradiction that immediately confronts the analyst who begins to model himself—to take his lead from or use as formative precursor—the pre-oedipal mother. What one learns from this mother—from observing her—is something that cannot be taught. The return is a cul-de-sac. There is no beginning, only the analysis of the fantasies of beginnings, of their wishful improvisation. It is as though, for the analyst, in practice there are two temptations, two extremes: identification either as caricature, playing mothers, or as the willing victim of an open transference; either guru or blank page.

It is not surprising that, faced with the impasse of the pre-oedipal mother, Bion and Winnicott promote, in different ways, the value of not-knowing in the analyst. Because the one who apparently knows at the deepest level, but perhaps without having been taught, is the pre-oedipal mother, the sphinx without a riddle. When the psychoanalytic theorist becomes wary of his omniscience he tends to make a fetish of "not knowing." "In short," Bion writes, "there is an inexhaustible fund of ignorance to draw upon—it is about all we do have to draw upon."[8] The skeptic always boasts.

If, in psychoanalysis, the method is inspiring but the formulated aims are by definition spurious, what are we left with if the analyst is mother? Psychic progress along developmental lines (Anna Freud); the secure internalization of the good object (Klein); achievement, however precarious, of the Depressive Position (Klein and Bion); a virtual True Self destiny (Winnicott). There is, I think, an inevitable connection between the analyst already in position as the mother—and especially the pre-oedipal mother—and psychoanalysis as the coercion or simulation of normality. And this is the situation, traditionally, when Dionysos arrives.[9]

Using a fantasy about mothers—about the beginning—to foreclose the transference turns psychoanalysis into perversion, perversion in the only meaningful sense of the term: knowing too exactly what one wants, the disavowal of contingency, omniscience as the cheating of time; the mother who, because she knows what's best for us, has nothing to offer.

- 11 -

Psychoanalysis and Idolatry

> Abraham falls victim to the following illusion: he cannot
> stand the uniformity of this world. Now the world is
> known, however, to be uncommonly various, which
> can be verified at any time by taking a handful of world
> and looking at it closely. Thus this complaint at the
> uniformity of the world is really a complaint at not hav-
> ing been mixed profoundly enough with the diversity
> of the world.
>
> Franz Kafka, *Parables and Paradoxes*

Anyone who goes to the Freud museum is immediately struck
by Freud's collection of antiquities, and particularly, perhaps,
by the forest of figurines from various cultures, on Freud's
desk. Freud, as the analyst, would sit overseeing them as he
listened to the patient from behind the couch; and the patient
lying on the couch could see them by turning to the right but
could not, of course, see Freud. In the first psychoanalytic setting—the paradigm of every psychoanalytic consulting room—
the patient could not see the analyst but could see his idols.

Clearly, for many reasons, entering Freud's consulting
room would have been an unusual experience; the Wolf-man
was reminded, he wrote, "not of a doctor's office but rather of
an archaeological study. Here were all kinds of statuettes and
other unusual objects which even the layman recognised as
archaeological finds from ancient Egypt."[1] Psychoanalysis, of
course, always takes place in a museum—and for the more
idolatrous, usually in the Freud museum—but the museum, the
stored past, comes to life in language and loses its fixity.

Hans Sachs, one of the early members of Freud's Wednesday Psychological Society in Vienna, recalls in his memoir how
"under the silent stare of idols and animal-shaped gods we listened to some new article by Freud, or read and discussed our
own products, or just talked about things that interested us."[2]

Presumably, the irony of the situation was not lost on them. And since Jewish thought, by definition, sets itself against idolatry, we should take this as one of the important scenes in the history of psychoanalysis: a group of Jewish men, in a room full of idols, having a new kind of conversation about sexuality. Even though they thought of themselves as secular Jews, it was the equivalent of putting a moustache on the *Mona Lisa*. It was a critique of traditional forms of reverence; because to talk about sexuality, from a psychoanalytic point of view, was to talk about the nature of belief. As the conventions of love poetry have always insisted, it is in our erotic life that we return, so to speak, to idolatry. And our erotic life—as psychoanalysis would reveal in quite unexpected ways—is intimately connected to our acquisitive, materialistic life.

Toward the end of the nineteenth century, in the major European capitals, it was possible to purchase gods. "The ancient gods still exist," Freud wrote to his friend Fliess in 1899, "for I have bought one or two lately, among them a stone Janus, who looks down on me with his two faces in a very superior fashion." [3] You know the gods still exist, Freud jokes, because you can buy them. They have become a new kind of commodity, just as the personal past was becoming something one could buy in the form of psychoanalysis. Certainly, recent archaeological discoveries had given vivid form to the idea that the dead do not disappear. And Janus, we may remember, the Roman god of gods, was the opener and closer of all things, who looked inward and outward, before and after; a pertinent god to have acquired given Freud's newfound preoccupations at the turn of the century.

It is, of course, tendentious to refer to what Freud called his "grubby old gods" as idols. In his collection of more than two thousand pieces there were many representations of deities, but Freud did not worship them. He simply collected them with some relish and obviously prized them very highly; although it would not be wildly speculative, from a psychoanalytic point of view, to infer that there were powerful unconscious identifications at work both with the people who had worshipped them and the people who had found them. If, as has been suggested, they also represented his family romance—his wishful allegiance to alternative cultures—then they were also a rather grandiose parody of the idea. It would not be a *family* romance that could contain Greek, Roman, Egyptian, Near Eastern, and Asian members, so much as a world-historical romance. "I have made many sacrifices," he writes to Stephan Zweig, and it is a telling phrase, "for my collection of Greek, Roman and Egyptian antiquities, and actually have read more archaeology than psychology."[4] He couldn't, of course, have had comparable Jewish antiquities, because there could be no such thing.

It is an irony, then, of some interest that psychoanalysis—in which only words and money are exchanged, in which no graven images are used, and which is carried out in an atmosphere of relative abstinence—had its beginnings in a setting populated by old gods. Freud's consulting room, in other words, was a rather vivid representation of an old dilemma: How many gods if any, and what are they for? None of Freud's antiquities were kept in his living quarters. So what was Freud telling his patients and himself by displaying his collection in the rooms where he practiced psychoanalysis, a theory and a therapy that was consistently an impassioned critique of religious belief? Certainly these antiquities in a Jewish doctor's consulting room articulated two things about culture, which had interesting implications for the new science of psychoanalysis. First, that culture was history, and that this history, which was of extraordinary duration, could be preserved and thought about. The present could be a cover story for the past. And second—and more threatening to the monotheism of a putatively chosen people—that culture was plural. These figurines from such diverse cultures, which represented what Freud called "the splendid diversity of human life," "the varied types of perfection," might suggest that the only viable notion of True Belief was of something local, provisional, and various. The figurines underlined the fact that there are all sorts of cultural conventions and worlds elsewhere, as many as can be found.

Much has been made of Freud, rightly, as a post-Enlighten-ment man of his time, committed to progress under the aegis of science, and to a critique of religion as enslavement through superstition. Freud was convinced that cultures, like individuals, developed from infantile, primitive magic to mature rational science, insofar as they were able to. What is less often spelled out is that Freud was obsessed by the notion of belief. Both magic and science, hysteria and common human unhappiness, delusion and psychoanalytic theory, he began to realize, could be described as questions of belief. As Freud famously wrote in his conclusion to the Schreber case: "It remains for the future to decide whether there is more delusion in my theory than I should like to admit, or whether there is more truth in Schreber's delusion that other people are yet able to believe."[5] The psycho-analytic question becomes not, Is that true? but What in your personal history disposes you to believe that? And *that,* of course, could be psychoanalytic theory. In other words, from a psychoanalytic point of view, belief changes from being a question about the qualities of the object of belief, to a question about the history of the subject, the believer. What is the uncon-scious problem that your belief solves for you, or the wishes that it satisfies? In therapy it is always an interesting question to ask someone in a state of conviction, What kind of person would you be if you no longer believed that? A symptom, of course, is always a state of conviction.

Despite Freud's endless disclaimers—his descriptions of himself, in one form or another, as a "godless Jew"—in his work the Jewish boundary, if I can put it like that, between idolatry and something else we might call True Belief, was recontested. The distinction that had organized Judaism became blurred as Freud used psychoanalysis to redescribe the roots of belief.

It makes sense to preserve faulty points of view for pos-sible future use.

Paul Feyerabend, *Farewell to Reason*

Freud's preoccupation with Moses is obviously relevant in this context (there are, incidentally, only two references to Aaron in Freud's work, one of which is a quotation from Eduard Meyer in a footnote, and neither of which even alludes to the Golden Calf). His interest in Moses, as many people have pointed out, was based in part on his identification with him both as an interpreter and as an abolisher of idols. In his first study of the patriarch, *The Moses of Michelangelo* (1914), Freud tries to describe his internal reactions to the Moses idolized, so to speak, in Michelangelo's famous sculpture: "In 1913, through three lonely September weeks, I stood daily in the church in front of the statue, studied it, measured it, drew it, until that understanding came to me that I only dared to express anonymously in the paper."[6] There is, of course, a certain irony in Freud's devotion to this idol, in Rome, of a man whose project was the destruction of idolatry. When Ernest Jones went to Rome in 1913 Freud wrote to him: "I envy you for seeing Rome so soon and so early in life. Bring my deepest devotion to Moses and write me about him." Jones replied obediently: "My first pilgrimage the day after my arrival was to convey your greetings to Moses, and I think he unbent a little from his haughtiness."[7] It is not obvious whom the joke was on.

But Freud was drawn irresistibly to this statue partly to understand why he was so drawn to it; why, that is to say, he seemed, quite unconsciously, to have made it into an idol: "No piece of statuary," he wrote in his essay,

> has ever made a stronger impression on me than this. How often have I mounted the steep steps of the unlovely Corso Cavour to the lonely place where the deserted church stands, and have essayed to support the angry scorn of the hero's glance. Sometimes I have crept cautiously out of the half-gloom of the interior as though I myself belonged to the mob upon whom his eye is turned—the mob which can hold fast no conviction, which has neither faith nor patience and which rejoices when it has regained its illusory idols.[8]

Freud, in this curious scene, half-identifies with the idolaters, the "mob," as he calls them contemptuously, which has "neither faith nor patience." Freud may be guilty of abandoning the religion of his fathers, but that wouldn't necessarily place him, a man of science, in Aaron's party, having to withstand "the angry scorn of the hero's glance." In this context perhaps, if you are not a Jew you are an idolater, but what are Freud's "illusory idols" that he creeps cautiously out of the church to return to? It would be glib simply to say that his idols are now Science and Psychoanalysis; but it is his psychoanalytic method that he returns to and uses to understand what we might call his transference to Michelangelo's *Moses*. And his interpretation of the statue, which his essay explains, is particularly interesting in the light of these considerations.

Freud is preoccupied by two things about Michelangelo's *Moses*. First, what is Moses' mood, the state of mind that Michelangelo has tried to represent? And second, at what point in the story is Moses portrayed? Reviewing the evidence of previous scholars, Freud begins by accepting what was then the traditional interpretation of the statue—Michelangelo shows Moses at the moment when he first sees his people worshipping the Golden Calf, the moment just before his rage. But then Freud, after his own analysis, comes up with an alternative construction. Actually, he proposes, the artist has shown Moses *after* his rage, in a state of recovery; that is, after the idolatry of his people has to be included in the story: not the moment of discovery, but the immediate period of realization. And this, Freud says, is what is so compelling for him about *Moses:* "What we see before us is not the inception of a violent action, but the remains of a movement that has already taken place. In his first transport of fury Moses desired to act, to spring up and take vengeance and forget the Tables; but he has overcome the temptation, and he will now remain seated and still in his frozen wrath and in his pain mingled with contempt."[9] If Freud, in this highly charged scenario, finds himself identifying with the idolatrous mob, he also admires Moses because of his self-control. He is an object of emulation for Freud because he does not take quick revenge on the idolaters; he suffers their difference.

This essay of Freud's, written in 1913, clearly also refers implicitly to C. G. Jung's defection; ironically, in this parallel Jung becomes the idolater, fleeing from Freud's devotion, so to speak, to sexuality. But the essay also has an intrapsychic significance that tells us something about Freud himself. It describes an internal configuration that is dramatized throughout Freud's work. That is to say, a relationship is described between an inner authority that organizes and defines, and a less developed, nonheroic, idolatrous mob that is impatient and unwilling to believe in the hero. The mob is skeptical and restive, and the hero has conviction. The hero, from the mob's point of view, is excessively demanding; the mob, from the hero's point of view, is immature, especially in its impatience. A misleadingly neat set of equations suggests itself: Moses as the superego, Aaron as the ego, and the idolatrous mob as the id. In Freud's redescription of Exodus, idolatry is infantile; it signifies a failure of renunciation. But Freud's interpretation of Michelangelo's *Moses* suggests that Freud is trying to contain— to keep alive in himself—the *relationship* between the Moses figure and the idolaters.

Returning to Moses twenty years later in his weird and wonderful book *Moses and Monotheism,* Freud gives final form to the possible virtues—the developmental achievement—that in his view distinguish Moses and his religion from what he contemptuously calls the "mob." In crude terms it is fair to say that Freud reduces all religious belief to the longing for the father: "A child's earliest years," he writes, "are dominated by an enormous overvaluation of his father," and this gets transferred on to a deity.[10] But in *Moses and Monotheism* we find—amid much fascinating and bizarre speculation—both an enthusiastic defense of monotheism and a profound ambivalence toward it. And this ambivalence reflects the child's ambivalence about both the father and the religion of the fathers, but also Freud's ambivalence about the version of adulthood generated by psychoanalysis.

Monotheism, for example—which he explicitly links with imperialism—in Freud's view produces intolerance. "Along with the belief in a single god," he writes, "religious intolerance was inevitably born, which had previously been alien to the ancient world and remained so long afterwards."[11] There is clearly an idealization of the ancient world here, but it is nevertheless worth bearing in mind that in what Freud calls the "ancient world" there were a large number of deities of both sexes, and that the gods of the classical ancient world were hedonists. And this point is not incidental, because for Freud, in *Moses and Monotheism,* monotheism seems to represent a triumph of the mind, or what Freud calls the "intellect," over the body. And this, Freud tries to say, but with considerable misgivings, is its great virtue. "For various reasons," he apparently once remarked to Ernest Jones, "the Jews have undergone a one-sided development and admire brains more than bodies."[12]

In what may now seem to us to be a questionable distinction, it is as if the body produces and worships idols, and the intellect produces the sublimated rigors of monotheism, what Freud calls the "heights of sublime abstraction." On the one hand he criticizes monotheism for its intolerance of other people, and on the other hand he praises it for its intolerance of the body. There is bodily clamor, and there is restraint. And for those like Moses and other chosen people who have managed what Freud calls this "triumph of intellectuality over sensuality"—this abstinence—there is one rather dubious reward. "All such advances in intellectuality," he writes, "have as their consequence that the individual's self-esteem is increased, that he is made proud—so that he feels *superior* to other people who have remained under the spell of sensuality." Now it is children, of course—whom Freud places in his alarming nineteenth-century category with women, neurotics, and "primitive races"—who remain under the spell of sensuality.[13] It is they who are prone to idolatry; but by the same token, in Freud's terms, they do not get their sexual excitement from feeling superior to other people.

A believer is bound to the teachings of religion by certain
ties of affection.

Sigmund Freud, *The Future of an Illusion*

From a psychoanalytic point of view, to talk about religion and
to talk about sexuality are to talk about childhood. And childhood begins, at least, "under the spell of sensuality." Throughout his writings Freud is extremely interested in this spell—both
in how resilient it was, and in what broke it, or rather, modified
it. Like adults in analysis, and for the same reasons, children
were seen to be extremely resistant when it came to relinquish-
ing pleasures. In his late essay "Analysis Terminable and Interminable" (1937)—one that is markedly skeptical about the
therapeutic efficacy of psychoanalysis—Freud offers as an
example telling children the so-called facts of life:

> After such enlightenment, children know something that
> they did not know before, but they make no use of the
> new knowledge that has been presented to them. We
> come to see that they are not even in so great a hurry to
> sacrifice for this new knowledge the sexual theories
> which might be described as a natural growth and which
> they have constructed in harmony with, and dependence
> on, their imperfect libidinal organisation—theories
> about the part played by the stork, about the nature of
> sexual intercourse and about the way in which babies are
> made. For a long time after they have been given sexual
> enlightenment they behave like primitive races who have
> had Christianity thrust upon them and who continue to
> worship their idols in secret.[14]

It is surely one of Freud's greatest contributions to have multi-
plied the possibilities for irony. Once again we find here complicated and ironic identifications at work. In what sense, for
example, are the facts of life—the scientific facts of life—like
Christianity? Freud made no secret of his views about Christianity—and particularly his contempt for Catholicism—and
yet, albeit figuratively, Christianity is being used here to represent the truth about sex. It is not clear whether this is a parody

of Truth or of Christianity. And the history, which Freud knew only too well, made it abundantly obvious that it wasn't only "primitive races" that Christians had wanted to convert; they had wanted to convert the Jews, who were, of course, notorious in anti-Semitic propaganda for their sexual preoccupations. If Freud is showing us, in this example, the conflict between Christianity and infantile sexuality, then we need to remember that Freud thought of himself as the discoverer of infantile sexuality, of the significance of infantile sexual theories in adult life; and that his work was, among many other things, a fierce critique of Christianity.

Children, he writes here, confronted with the Truth, "make no use of the new knowledge" but "continue to worship their idols in secret." And their idols are theories; like psychoanalysis, theories about sexuality. Freud, in this example, as a man of science must, ironically, side with the Christian missionaries; but his sympathies are manifestly with the refusal by the idolatrous children, whose sexual theories he refers to as a "natural growth." In other words, we find once again in Freud, as we did in his accounts of Moses, the generosity of a split identification. He has internalized the ancient Jewish struggle between idolatry and True Belief; and in each of these instances True Belief involves submission to a more powerful authority. The truth becomes something we give in to, something with which we have a sadomasochistic relationship.

In *The Future of an Illusion* (1927), his most sustained investigation into the personal origins of religious belief, Freud defines religious ideas as "teachings and assertions about facts and conditions of external (or internal) reality which tells one something one has not discovered for oneself and which lay claim to one's belief." Religious ideas, in other words, are imposed, not found. And clearly, as always in Freud's writing, there is an implicit parallel being drawn with psychoanalytic ideas; the question being not, Are they true? but Why do you believe them? Children, as in the previous example, discover their sexual theories for themselves, according to their developmental capacity; the adults don't inform them that one makes babies by kissing. A distinction is being made here by Freud that we are more familiar with from later object-relations theory; that is, the distinction between an object that can be found, and an object that is forced upon us. And pleasure, we should remember in this context, unlike pain, cannot be forced upon us.

Freud asks—in the sometimes reductive generalizations in *The Future of an Illusion*—what kind of objects are religious beliefs, and what are they used for? And he answers that they are paternal objects, which we invest with power and authority to console us for our original and pervasive helplessness. In fact, in Freud's terms, we don't believe, we wish; and above all we wish to believe. Because of our formative helplessness, every belief, we think, protects us from something. And in this sense a belief, for Freud, is like a symptom; we imagine that a catastrophe will ensue if we relinquish it. And again, like a symptom, religious belief, Freud says, is a way of not leaving home. Anyone who has been able to relinquish what he calls the "religious illusion" will "be in the same position as a child who has left the parental house where he is so warm and comfortable . . . Men cannot remain children for ever; they must in the end go out into hostile life. We may call this 'education to reality.' " [15] Reality, we must infer from this, is that which cannot be wishfully improved; something we could, perhaps, call Nature. [16]

For Freud, it is the element of wish-fulfillment that makes all religious belief a childish illusion. Something called "reality" now fills the space that was once inhabited by the monotheism of Moses. And this reality is ineluctable, like death; all belief is now idolatry, and idolatry is an anaesthetic. The believer, Freud insists, is like an addict, and "the effect of religious consolations may be likened to that of a narcotic," a "sleeping draught." Religion is simply an elaborate acknowledgment of what Freud calls "the perplexity and helplessness of the human race," but it is a "bitter-sweet poison." [17] It is all very simple. The child believes in the father—although exactly what the child believes about the father is not spelled out—and the adult, in the same way, believes in his god because he is too frightened to grow up. But why is Freud, as many people have noticed, when he tells his own story about religion, so unusually, indeed excessively, hostile to it? If it is so obvious what Religion, in the abstract, really is, why does he have to keep telling us? He disparages religious belief in a way that he has taught us to interpret; so we can ask a simple question: What is the doubt he is trying to stifle by his overinsistent critique?

One of the doubts, I think, was that he was talking not only about religion. About two-thirds of the way through *The Future of an Illusion* Freud begins to realize that he may be using religion as a pretext to talk about belief. And this had interesting implications for psychoanalysis, because Freud had developed a treatment that made use of this infantile capacity for belief. Transference, after all, is a form of secular idolatry. Just as Freud was manifestly uncertain as to what there was beyond transference, so he begins to doubt, again, in *The Future of an Illusion,* whether there is any essential or discernible difference between idolatry and true belief, and whether any area of our lives can be anything other than what he calls illusion. "May not other cultural assets," he writes, "of which we hold a high opinion and by which we let our lives be ruled be of a similar nature? Must not the assumptions that determine our political regulations be called illusions as well? And is it not the case that in our civilisation the relations between the sexes are disturbed by an erotic illusion or a number of such illusions?" [18] And what of psychoanalysis itself, which Freud noticeably fails to mention, but of which he, and some of us, hold a high opinion even if we don't let our lives be ruled by it?

Through psychoanalysis Freud suddenly seems to have collapsed the traditional opposition between idolatry and true belief. And he had certainly, of course, described an unconscious that was the antithesis of an idol, that could not be worshipped and should not be idealized. If all belief is idolatory, and even Moses was childish, what then is the alternative? And the answer, Freud states emphatically, in the conclusion to *The Future of an Illusion,* is science; because in science, unlike our wishful illusions, our beliefs are subject to correction. This could, of course, be the most ironic wish of all; a wish that our wishes be correctable. But from one of Freud's many points of view, potential objects of belief were to be replaced by a method of inquiry into the personal history of belief.

The analyst, Lacan says, is the one who is supposed to know, but it is a false belief. So we are left with a paradox that is integral to our present subject. With the discovery of transference Freud evolved what could be called a cure by idolatry; in fact, potentially, a cure of idolatry, through idolatry. But the one thing psychoanalysis cannot cure, when it works, is belief in psychoanalysis. And that is a problem.

Notes

Introduction

1. Sigmund Freud, *Studies on Hysteria,* with Josef Breuer, *The Standard Edition of the Complete Psychological Works of Sigmund Freud,* 24 vols., ed. James Strachey, trans. in collaboration with Anna Freud (London: Hogarth Press and the Institute of Psycho-Analysis, 1953–1974; hereafter cited as Freud, *SE*), II, p. 305.
2. See *Pragmatism's Freud: The Moral Disposition of Psychoanalysis,* ed. Joseph H. Smith and William Kerrigan (Baltimore: Johns Hopkins University Press, 1986), p. 7.
3. W. H. Auden, *The Dyer's Hand* (London: Faber, 1963), p. 6.
4. Adam Zagajewski, "Ode to Plurality," in *Tremor: Selected Poems* (New York: Farrar, Straus and Giroux, 1985). For a brilliant discussion of psychoanalysis as an oppressively coercive reading of a putative human subject see Mark Edmundson, *Towards Reading Freud* (Princeton: Princeton University Press, 1990).

1. On Tickling

1. For an explanation of Winnicott's concept of holding, see page 44.
2. Freud, *Three Essays on the Theory of Sexuality, SE* VII, p. 183.

2. First Hates

1. William James, *Psychology: The Briefer Course,* ed. Gordon Allport (Notre Dame, Ind.: University of Notre Dame Press, 1985), p. 275.
2. Ibid., p. 281.
3. Ibid., p. 279.
4. William James, *Pragmatism* (Cambridge, Mass.: Harvard University Press, 1975), pp. 281, 98.
5. See André Green, "Passions and Their Vicissitudes," in *On Private Madness* (London: Hogarth Press, 1986), pp. 214–253.
6. William James, *Talks on Psychology and Life's Ideals* (London: Longman's, 1899), p. 264.
7. Freud, *Inhibitions, Symptoms and Anxiety, SE* XX, p. 168.
8. Ibid., p. 190.
9. Quoted in *Drawings by Bonnard* (London: Arts Council of Great Britain Publications, 1984), p. 16.

10. See Julia Kristeva, "Something to Be Scared of," in *Powers of Horror* (New York: Columbia University Press, 1982), pp. 32–55.

11. Roger Money-Kyrle, *The Collected Papers of Money-Kyrle* (Perthshire: Clunie Press, 1978), p. 60.

12. Donald Davidson, "Paradoxes of Irrationality," in *Philosophical Essays on Freud*, ed. R. Wollheim and J. Hopkins (Cambridge: Cambridge University Press, 1982), p. 303.

13. Freud, "Negation," *SE* XIX, p. 237; idem, "Instincts and Their Vicissitudes," *SE* XIV, p. 136.

3. On Risk and Solitude

1. Freud, *Introductory Lectures on Psycho-Analysis, SE* XVI, p. 407.

2. Ibid., p. 399.

3. Ibid., *SE* XV, p. 153.

4. Jacques Lacan, "The Direction of the Treatment and the Principles of Its Power," in *Ecrits* (London: Tavistock, 1977), p. 254.

5. Letter to Charles Cotton from his patron Lord Halifax, in *Montaigne's Essays*, trans. Charles Cotton (London: Ward Lock, 1700), p. 5.

6. Iris Murdoch, *Sartre* (London: Chatto & Windus, 1987), pp. 36–37.

7. D. W. Winnicott, *Deprivation and Delinquency* (London: Tavistock, 1984), p. 147.

8. Ibid.

9. D. W. Winnicott, "Primitive Emotional Development," in *Through Paediatrics to Psychoanalysis* (London: Hogarth Press, 1975), p. 152.

10. Stephen Mitchell, *Relational Concepts in Psychoanalysis* (Cambridge, Mass.: Harvard University Press, 1988), p. 32.

11. D. W. Winnicott, "Psychoanalysis and the Sense of Guilt," *The Naturational Processes and the Facilitating Environment* (London: Hogarth Press, 1965), p. 15. For discussion of the morality of object-relations theory, see Adam Phillips, "Besides Good and Evil," *Winnicott Studies* 6 (1991), 14–19.

12. Winnicott, "Psychoanalysis and the Sense of Guilt," pp. 23–24.

13. Ibid., p. 24.

14. Ibid., p. 26; *Oxford English Dictionary*, s.v.

15. Winnicott, "Psychoanalysis and the Sense of Guilt," p. 26.

16. Ibid.

17. D. W. Winnicott, "The Use of an Object," in *Playing and Reality* (London: Tavistock, 1971), p. 106. For illuminating contemporary discussion of the making real—the discovery of the subjectivity—of the object, see in particular Emmanuel Ghent, "Masochism, Submission, Surrender," *Contemporary Psychoanalysis* 26, no. 1 (January 1990), 108–136; and Jessica Benjamin, *The Bonds of Love* (New York: Pantheon Books, 1988).

18. Winnicott, "Psychoanalysis and the Sense of Guilt," p. 26
19. Maurice Blanchot, "The Essential Solitude," in *The Gaze of Orpheus,* trans. Lydia Davis (Barrytown, N.Y.: Station Hill Press, 1981), pp. 63–77.
20. Friedrich Nietzsche, *Daybreak,* trans. R. J. Hollingdale (Cambridge: Cambridge University Press, 1982), p. 201.
21. Masud Khan, "Infancy, Aloneness, and Madness," in *Hidden Selves* (London: Hogarth Press, 1983), p. 181.

4. On Composure

1. Freud, *Beyond the Pleasure Principle, SE* XVIII, p. 27.
2. See Jean Laplanche, *Life and Death in Psychoanalysis* (Baltimore: Johns Hopkins Press, 1976).
3. D. W. Winnicott, "The Mind and Its Relation to the Psyche-Soma," in *Through Paediatrics to Psychoanalysis* (London: Hogarth Press, 1975), p. 244.
4. Ibid., p. 246.
5. Ibid.
6. Georg Groddeck, *The Unknown Self* (London: Vision Press, 1951), p. 46. Lacan's mirror-stage is pertinent here. I take the child's delight at seeing itself cohere in a mirror image as a reaction-formation to deal with the terror of seeing itself unified into an image and ripe for naming. The child has a fear, as well as a wish, of being collected into a parcel and made ready to be passed around.

5. Worrying and Its Discontents

1. See Wilfred Bion, *Seven Servants* (New York: Jason Aronson, 1977).
2. D. W. Winnicott, *Deprivation and Delinquency* (London: Tavistock, 1984), pp. 126, 128.
3. Freud, *Beyond the Pleasure Principle, SE* XVIII, p. 32.
4. Freud, *The Unconscious, SE* XIV, p. 186.
5. See Rodney Needham, *Belief, Language and Experience* (Oxford: Blackwell, 1972).

6. Returning the Dream

1. Freud, *Female Sexuality, SE* XXI, p. 231.
2. D. W. Winnicott, "Communicating and Not Communicating Leading to a Study of Certain Opposites," in *The Maturational Processes and the Facilitating Environment* (London: Hogarth Press, 1965), p. 187.
3. Masud Khan, *The Privacy of the Self* (London: Hogarth Press, 1974), p. 304.

4. Masud Khan, *Alienation in Perversions* (London: Hogarth Press, 1979), p. 213.

5. Ibid., p. 214.

6. Freud, quoted in J.-B. Pontalis, *Frontiers in Psychoanalysis* (London: Hogarth Press, 1981), p. 33.

7. Masud Khan, "Dream Psychology and the Evolution of the Psychoanalytic Situation," in *The Privacy of the Self*, pp. 27–41; idem, "The Use and Abuse of Dream in Psychic Experience," ibid., pp. 306–315; idem, "Beyond the Dreaming Experience," in *Hidden Selves* (London: Hogarth Press, 1983), pp. 42–50.

8. Khan, "Dream Psychology," p. 29.

9. Masud Khan, "Infancy, Aloneness, and Madness," in *Hidden Selves* (London: Hogarth Press, 1983), p. 181; Pontalis, *Frontiers,* p. 33.

10. Khan, "Use and Abuse of Dream," p. 305.

11. Vincent Descombes, *Objects of All Sorts* (Oxford: Blackwell, 1985), p. 28.

12. Khan, "Beyond the Dreaming Experience," p. 50.

13. Ibid., p. 46.

14. Quoted in Khan, "Beyond the Dreaming Experience," p. 45.

15. Khan, "Dream Psychology," p. 40.

16. Khan, "Use and Abuse of Dream," p. 315.

17. Khan, "Beyond the Dreaming Experience," p. 49.

18. Khan, *Alienation in Perversions,* p. 9.

19. Marion Milner, *The Hands of the Living God* (London: Virago, 1988), p. xxxi.

20. Khan, "Beyond the Dreaming Experience," p. 49.

21. Ibid., p. 183.

22. John Wisdom, *Philosophy and Psychoanalysis* (Oxford: Blackwell, 1953), p. 167. For an account of the relationship between acknowledgment and nonappropriation, see Christopher Benfey's brilliant *Emily Dickinson and the Problem of Others* (Amherst: University of Massachusetts Press, 1984).

7. On Being Bored

1. Freud, *Mourning and Melancholia, SE* XIV, pp. 245–246.

2. D. W. Winnicott, "The Observation of Infants in a Set Situation," in *Through Paediatrics to Psychoanalysis* (London: Hogarth Press, 1975), pp. 52–53, 66.

3. Ibid., pp. 53–54.

4. Ibid., pp. 58–59.

5. In D. W. Winnicott, *Deprivation and Delinquency* (London: Tavistock, 1984), pp. 120–131.

6. See Melanie Klein, "Notes on Some Schizoid Mechanisms," in *The Selected Melanie Klein*, ed. Juliet Mitchell (Harmondsworth: Penguin, 1986), pp. 176–200.

7. See Jean Laplanche, *Life and Death in Psychoanalysis* (Baltimore: Johns Hopkins Press, 1976).

8. Freud, "Fetishism," *SE* XXI, p. 154.

9. See Joyce McDougall, *Plea for a Measure of Abnormality* (New York: International Universities Press, 1980), for an extended discussion of the uses of fetishism to disavow meaning and perception.

10. Christopher Bollas, "The Transformational Object," in *The Shadow of the Object: Psychoanalysis of the Unthought Known* (London: Free Associations, 1987), p. 14.

11. Marcel Proust, *Swann's Way*, trans. Terence Kilmartin (London: Hogarth Press, 1981), pp. 47–48.

8. Looking at Obstacles

1. Jean-Paul Sartre, *Being and Nothingness*, trans. Hazel E. Barnes (London: Methuen, 1957), p. 488.

2. Jean-Jacques Rousseau, *Confessions*, trans. J. M. Cohen (Harmondsworth: Penguin, 1953), p. 45.

3. Freud, *Jokes and Their Relation to the Unconscious*, *SE* VIII, p. 101.

4. Marcel Proust, *Within a Budding Grove*, trans. Terence Kilmartin (London: Hogarth Press, 1981), bk. 1, p. 621.

5. Sandor Ferenczi and Otto Rank, *The Development of Psycho-Analysis*, trans. Newton (New York: International Universities Press, 1986), p. 15.

6. Freud, "Fetishism," *SE* XXI, p. 155.

7. Victor Smirnoff, *Psychoanalysis in France*, ed. D. Widlocher and S. Lebovici (New York: International Universities Press, 1980), p. 324.

8. Freud, "Fetishism," p. 154.

9. Ibid., p. 156. It may be more useful, for example, to talk of link envy as well as, or instead of, penis envy, children of both sexes envying the parents' unique capacity for connection with and access to each other via the genitals.

10. D. W. Winnicott, "Transitional Objects and Transitional Phenomena," in *Through Paediatrics to Psychoanalysis* (London: Hogarth Press, 1975), pp. 233–234.

11. Peter Winch, *Simone Weil: "The Just Balance"* (Cambridge: Cambridge University Press, 1989), p. 66.

12. Freud, *The Unconscious*, *SE* XIV, p. 186.

13. John Cage, *For the Birds* (London: Marion Boyers, 1981), p. 40.

9. Plotting for Kisses

1. Sandor Ferenczi, *Final Contributions to the Problems of Psychoanalysis* (London: Hogarth Press, 1955), p. 219.
2. Freud, *Analysis Terminable and Interminable, SE* XXIII, p. 234.
3. D. W. Winnicott, *Through Paediatrics to Psychoanalysis* (London: Hogarth Press, 1958), p. 41.
4. Freud, *Introductory Lectures on Psycho-Analysis, SE* XVI, p. 322.
5. Bob Dylan, *Lyrics 1962–1985* (London: Jonathan Cape, 1987), p. 140.
6. Freud, *Three Essays on the Theory of Sexuality, SE* VII, p. 182.
7. Robert Burton, *The Anatomy of Melancholy* (London: J. M. Dent, 1932), p. 111.

10. Playing Mothers

1. D. W. Winnicott, *Home Is Where We Start From* (Harmondsworth: Penguin, 1987), p. 123.
2. In "The Origins of Transference," for example, Klein writes: "The comfort and care given after birth, particularly the first feeding experiences, are felt to come from good forces" (*Collected Papers*, III [London: Hogarth Press, 1975], p. 239). These "good forces," in the mother and in the analyst as nonretaliatory object, are assumed to attenuate the "bad forces" of the Death Instinct.
3. Anna Freud, *Normality and Pathology in Childhood* (New York: International Universities Press, 1965), p. 168.
4. See Mikkel Borch-Jacobsen, *Lacan: The Absolute Master* (Stanford: Stanford University Press, 1991), for a persuasive recent discussion of the problem of identification vis-à-vis the putative aims of psychoanalysis. See also Lionel Trilling, *Freud and the Crisis of Our Culture* (Boston: Beacon Press, 1955), for a remarkably lucid and foresightful discussion of Freud's sense of what was "beyond" culture. Ignacio Matte-Blanco's *Thinking, Feeling and Being* (London: Routledge, 1988) must now be the canonical text for the relationship between identification and unconscious categories in psychoanalytic theory.
5. Wilfred Bion, *Second Thoughts* (Northvale, N.J.: Jason Aronson, 1967), p. 116.
6. D. W. Winnicott, *The Maturational Processes and the Facilitating Environment* (London: Hogarth Press, 1972), p. 167.
7. D. W. Winnicott, *Human Nature* (London: Free Association Books, 1988), pp. 119, 62.
8. Wilfred Bion, *Clinical Seminars and Four Papers* (Abingdon: Fleetwood Press, 1987), p. 244.
9. The *Bacchae* of Euripides is the paradigmatic text, but see also Marcel

Detienne's *Dionysos à ciel ouvert* (Paris: Hachette, 1986), translated as *Dionysos at Large* by Arthur Goldhammer (Cambridge, Mass.: Harvard University Press, 1989).

11. Psychoanalysis and Idolatry

1. Quoted in Peter Gay, *Freud: A Life for Our Time* (New York: W. W. Norton, 1988), pp. 170–171.
2. Hans Sachs, *Freud: Master and Friend* (London: Imago, 1945), p. 80.
3. *The Complete Letters of Sigmund Freud and Wilhelm Fliess*, trans. and ed. Jeffrey Masson (Cambridge, Mass.: Harvard University Press, 1985), p. 361.
4. Gay, *Freud*, pp. 170–171.
5. Freud, *The Case of Schreber*, SE XII, p. 79.
6. Freud, *The Moses of Michelangelo*, SE XIII, pp. 211–240.
7. Quoted in Gay, *Freud*, pp. 314–315.
8. Freud, *The Moses of Michelangelo*, p. 213.
9. Ibid., p. 229.
10. See Freud, *The Future of an Illusion*, SE XXI, pp. 5–58.
11. Freud, *Moses and Monotheism*, SE XXIII, p. 50.
12. Quoted in Gay, *Freud*, p. 599.
13. Freud, *Moses and Monotheism*, p. 115.
14. Freud, "Analysis Terminable and Interminable," SE XXIII, p. 234.
15. Freud, *The Future of an Illusion*, p. 49.
16. For a gloss on the word *Nature* see Camille Paglia, *Sexual Personae* (New Haven: Yale University Press, 1990).
17. Freud, *The Future of an Illusion*, p. 49.
18. Ibid., p. 34.

Credits

Earlier versions of five of the essays in this volume were published in *Raritan:* "On Tickling," 5, no. 4 (1985); "First Hates: Phobias in Theory," 11, no. 5 (1992); "On Composure," 6, no. 4 (1986); "Worrying and Its Discontents," 9, no. 2 (1989); and "On Being Bored," 6, no. 2 (1986). Earlier versions of seven essays were published in *Nouvelle Revue de Psychanalyse:* "On Tickling" (Spring 1985), "On Risk and Solitude" (Autumn 1987), "On Composure" (Autumn 1985), "Returning the Dream: In Memoriam Masud Khan" (Autumn 1989), "On Being Bored" (Autumn 1986), "Plotting for Kisses" (Autumn 1987), and "Playing Mothers: Between Pedagogy and Transference" (Spring 1992). "Psychoanalysis and Idolatry" was published as "Freud's Idols" in the *London Review of Books,* 27 September 1990.

The following have kindly granted permission to print segments of poetry:

John Berryman, "Dream Song 14": Faber and Faber Ltd;
   Farrar, Straus & Giroux
Bob Dylan, "Dirge": Jonathan Cape Ltd.
W. S. Graham, "The Hill of Intrusion": Nessie Graham
Ikkyu, *Crow with No Mouth:* Copper Canyon Press
Adam Zagajewski, "Ode to Plurality": Collins Harvill

Index

Absence: of mothers, 27, 28–29, 32, 75–76, 91; boredom and, 74, 75; of objects, 76, 78
Acknowledgment, 126n22
Adler, Alfred, 82
Adolescence, 33; objects and, 30–31; risks of, 30, 31, 32; sexuality in, 30, 31, 53, 94, 95, 96; solitude in, 32; worries and, 49; kissing and, 94, 95
Adorno, Theodor, 30
Adults and adulthood, 45, 49; tickling of children, 9–10; risks of, 30, 78; solitude in, 32; ruthlessness and, 39; boredom and, 68, 69–70, 75, 78; object seeking in, 77; desire and, 78; kissing and, 95; infantile sexuality and, 118; religious belief, 119–120
Aggression, 35, 54
Agoraphobia, 13–16
Aimlessness, 59, 60
All for Love (Dryden), 51
Ambivalence, 115
Analogy, 48, 87; used in psychoanalysis, 1–3, 4, 5, 106
Anal stage, 6
"Analysis Terminable and Interminable" (Freud), 117
Anatomy of Melancholy (Burton), 100
Anticipation, 69, 84
Antisocialness, 75
Anxiety, 16, 18, 28, 43, 52–53, 96
Art and artists, 2, 3, 5, 36–37, 39–40, 113–114
Artaud, Antonin, 60
Association, 47, 55–56, 66; free, 3, 15
Attention, free-floating, 69, 101
Auden, W. H., 7, 48
Authenticity, 4
Authority/power, 22, 45
Autoeroticism, 94
Autonomy, 22, 38

Bacon, Francis, 29
Being and Nothingness (Sartre), 81–82
Belief, 15, 110, 111, 112, 117, 119; as experience, 58; in objects, 59; true, 120; false, 121. *See also* Religion; True Belief
Benign circle, 36
Betrayal, 100
"Beyond the Dreaming Experience" (Freud), 64, 67
Beyond the Pleasure Principle (Freud), 43
Bion, Wilfred, 48, 103, 105–106, 107
Blanchot, Maurice, 40
Body, 41, 96; as object, 30, 40; representations of, 31, 32; composure of, 43; fantasy and, 43, 44; one-body relationship, 62; movement, 73, 74; of mother, 81; integrity of, 87; sucking of, 93, 94, 98; as mother substitute, 94; vs. intellect, 116
Bollas, Christopher, 76
Bonnard, Pierre, 19
Boredom, 5, 20, 68–78
Bowlby, John, 103
Breast, 34, 75; sucking of, 93–94, 97, 98–99; -infant relationship, 105–106
British School, 102, 103, 105

Cage, John, 92
"Capacity to Be Alone, The" (Winnicott), 63
Care, 31, 32, 34–41, 44, 45, 49
Castration, 16, 87, 88, 89. *See also* Penis
Catholicism, 117
Censorship, 53, 55, 64, 86
Charcot, Jean Martin, 103
Chekhov, Anton, 100
Children and childhood: tickling of, 9–10; stories of, 11; phobias, 15,

Children and childhood *(cont.)*
27, 79–80; memories, 17; risks, 27,
78; morality of, 35; solitude in, 41;
desire for mother, 43; excitement
and, 43; mental development, 44–
45; worries, 49; love, 59–60; boredom, 68–76; self-expression, 73–74;
construction of obstacles, 90–91;
sensuality/sexual theories, 116, 117,
118–119; idolatry, 118
Christianity, 117–118
Claustrophobia, 17
Compliance, 34
Composure, 42–46
Compulsion, repetition, 59, 86–87
Concern, 36, 37, 49, 96; for object,
33–34, 38, 39. *See also* Worrying
Confessions (Rousseau), 84
Conflict, 54–55
Conscious, 43, 91
Construction of obstacles, 80–81, 84–
85, 86, 87, 89, 90–91, 92
Continuity, 80
Control: omnipotent, 29–30, 38, 39,
48, 50; magical, 31; defensive, 44
Controversial Discussions, 104
Conversation, 49; psychoanalysis as,
1, 4, 6, 7–8
Conviction, 4
Cooperation, 35
Crabbe, George, 87
Creativity, 36–37, 39–40; of dreams,
55, 66
Culture, 4, 109, 111, 112, 120; lan-
guage games in, 8
Cure, 1–3, 26, 48, 82; self-, 42, 71
Curiosity, 2, 3, 6; phobias and, 14,
20, 23; perversion and, 63; boredom
and, 75; of infants, 95

Darwin, Charles, 9, 11, 13, 15, 98
Davidson, Donald, 23
Death, 18, 24, 27, 77, 90, 119; in
dreams, 28; of desire, 83; obstacles
to, 89; instinct, 128n2
Defenses, 76. *See also* Self: protection/
defense
Delusion, 112
Demands, 58, 61, 62, 69–70
Dependency, 29, 41, 69

Depression, 36, 53
Depressive Position, 107
Descombes, Vincent, 65
Desire(s), 11, 52, 55, 58, 73, 103; fear
and, 12–13, 16–17, 18; exchange of,
14; memory and, 16, 40; projection
of, 16–17; ego and, 24, 43, 75;
solitude and, 29; of infants and
children, 34, 36, 39, 45–46, 64,
71, 72, 74; of mother, 45–46;
perversions and, 66; wishes and, 68,
69, 91; simulation of, 70–71;
unconscious, 71, 83; preconditions
for, 74–75; boredom and, 76, 78;
obstacles and, 82–85, 92; satisfaction of, 100
Despair/desolation, 71
Destruction, 37, 39, 76, 89, 94
Development/developmental theory,
11, 30, 33, 41, 49, 57, 60, 104;
psychoanalysis and, 6, 61–62, 105;
unconscious and, 7; sexual, 10, 94–
95, 96, 97–98, 99; phobias and, 25;
risks of, 38, 39; mental, 44, 45, 46,
88; dreams and, 64; emotional, 68,
69; obstacles and, 90, 92; of character, 93
Development of Psycho-Analysis, The
(Ferenczi/Rank), 86
Dialogue, 3
Dickens, Charles, 51
Difference, 62, 89–90, 115
Disappointment, 99
Disillusionment, 35, 67, 75, 99
Dissociation, 34, 45, 70, 88
Double-think, 76
Doubt, 54, 55, 58, 70, 92
Dream(s), 7, 27; -work, 10, 55, 64,
77; interpretation, 20, 56, 62, 64,
65, 66, 92; phobias and, 20–21;
unconscious and, 28, 57, 65, 66,
102; worries and, 47–48, 53, 55–58;
punishment, 54; creativity of, 55,
66; use of, in psychoanalysis, 61,
64, 65, 104; as text/experience, 64,
65, 66–67; good, 65, 66, 102;
-space, 66; day-, 77; obstacles to, 92
"Dream Psychology and the Evolution of the Psychoanalytic Situation" (Khan), 64

Eating and feeding, 36, 50–51, 54, 71, 91, 102; oral eroticism and, 93–94, 96, 97

Ego, 16, 72, 76, 115; desire and, 24, 43, 75; phobias and, 25; pure pleasure, 25; -psychology, 32; -ideal, 39; auxiliary, 63, 70; waking, 65; search for obstacles by, 92

Embarrassment, 95

Emotions, 48, 68, 69

Empiricism, 103

English Synonymes Explained (Crabbe), 87

Environment, 63; external (outside world), 24, 30, 32, 34, 98; internal, 40, 44, 46, 57; perfect, 46; holding, 60; for dreams, 66; testing of, 72; use of, 74

"Envy and Gratitude" (Klein), 38

Eros, 6

Eroticism, 10, 22, 52, 53, 100, 116; oral, 93–94, 96, 97; idolatry and, 110, 120. *See also* Sensuality; Sexuality

Erotogenic zones, 10–11, 97, 98

Estrangement technique, 102

Evolution, 13

Excitement, 9, 22, 42; of children and infants, 43, 45; erotic, 53, 116; obstacles and, 84–85

Experience, 14, 24, 58, 106; tickling as, 10, 11; fantasy of, 11; emotional, 48; of self, 62; dreams as, 64, 65, 66–67; waiting for (boredom), 68–69; repression of, 87

Expression of the Emotions in Man and Animals (Darwin), 9

Facts, The (Roth), 52

Fairbairn, Ronald, 103

Faith, 106

False Self, 34, 60, 70

Family, 81, 111

Fantasies, 4, 11, 15, 36, 38, 42, 46, 75; incestuous, 16; phobias and, 17–18, 23, 25, 80; of body, 43, 44; masturbation, 43, 50; of success, 54; of purpose, 57; object/subject relationship in, 59; wishes and, 59, 107; of greed, 71; of continuity, 80;

of mother, 88, 91, 104, 108; of kissing, 100; of function, 101–102

Fathers, 32, 41, 81, 87, 88, 115, 119

Fear, 14, 15, 32; of desire, 12–13, 16–17, 18; of castration, 16, 87, 88. *See also* Phobia(s)

Feelings, 50, 55, 73, 75, 78, 92, 95

Ferenczi, Sandor, 86, 93, 94, 97

Fetishism and fetishes, 76, 87–88, 89, 107

Fliess, Wilhelm, 14

Forgetting, 40, 57

Free association, 3, 15

Freedom, 39

Freud, Anna, 103, 104, 107

Freud, Sigmund, 33, 41, 44, 90; on psychoanalysis, 1–3, 32, 61, 102; devotion to science, 3, 5, 114, 118; theory of the unconscious, 3, 6, 7, 15, 54, 65, 91–92; sexual development theory, 10, 94–95, 96, 97–98, 99–100, 115; on desire, 12, 13; on phobias, 14, 15, 16–17, 22, 23, 24, 25, 27–28; on ego, 24, 43; on dreams, 40, 54, 55, 61, 65, 66, 77; on worrying, 50, 53, 54–55; on excess, 59, 60; on mourning, 71, 72; on jokes, 85, 110; on fetishism, 87–88; on mothering, 103–104; on idolatry, 109–111, 113–114, 115, 121; on religion, 112–113, 114, 115, 116–117, 118–120

Frustration, 11, 69, 93

Function, 101

Future, 14, 77, 112

Future of an Illusion, The (Freud), 118–119, 120

Games, 8, 11, 41, 91, 104

Gender, 105

Genitals, 87, 88, 96, 97, 127n9

Genius, 3

Good life, 4, 5, 6, 33

Greed, 71, 96

Green, André, 14

Groddeck, Georg, 46

Guilt, 35, 36, 37, 39, 54, 61

Hallucination, 34

Hate, 20, 24, 25, 38

Health, 40, 55, 57
Helplessness, 9, 10, 22, 69, 119
Hermeneutics, 65, 67
Hesitation, 72, 73, 74
Holding and holding function, 10, 14, 47, 105; of infant, 27, 31, 32, 38, 63, 107; of self, 30, 32, 44; defined, 44; failure of, 60; use of, in psychoanalysis, 65; of experience, 69; of mood, 70
Hostility, 30, 120
Human Nature (Winnicott), 107
Humiliation, 10
Humor, 4, 7. *See also* Jokes
Hunger, 9, 34, 71, 91. *See also* Eating and feeding
Hysteria, 1, 10, 43, 103, 112

Idealization, 3, 39, 120
Identity and identification, 101, 104–105, 118, 128n4; of psychoanalyst, 5, 63, 105; of patient, 6, 8, 63, 105
Idolatry, 109–121
Illness, 40
Illusion, 34, 91, 119, 120–121
Imagination, 6, 35, 42, 50, 54, 62
Improvisation, 2–3, 6
Incest, 16, 24, 83
Independence, 45
Infancy/infant(s), 33; absence of mother and, 27, 28–29, 32, 75–76, 91; holding environment and, 27, 31, 32, 38, 63, 107; solitude of, 28, 29–30, 31, 41, 62, 64, 69, 75–76; objects and, 31, 37; -mother relationship, 32, 34, 35, 44–45, 61, 62, 71, 81, 89, 103, 105–106; desires of, 34, 36, 39, 45–46, 64, 74; -in-care alone with himself, 41, 62; mental development, 44–45; satisfaction of, 66, 98, 99, 104; oral eroticism, 93–94, 95, 98, 99, 118; sucking and relation to breast, 93–94, 97, 98–99, 105–106; observation of, 104; psyche, 105
Inhibition, 73
Instincts, 6, 13, 36, 43, 67; wishes and, 54, 55; satisfaction of, 85
"Instincts and Their Vicissitudes" (Freud), 24

Integration, 44
Intellect, 45, 77, 116
Intelligibility, 6, 7
Interpretation: of dreams, 20, 56, 62, 64, 65, 66, 92; of phobias, 20; by analyst, 61, 62, 74; of transference, 106–107; of idols, 113
Intimacy, 34, 57, 58, 59, 60, 62
Introductory Lectures (Freud), 27–28
Irrationality, 12–13, 15, 23
Isolation, 4, 31, 46, 89

James, William, 12–13, 14, 15, 16, 19
Jokes, 7, 85–86, 110, 113. *See also* Laughter
Jokes and Their Relation to the Unconscious (Freud), 85
Jones, Ernest, 116
Judaism, 110, 112–113, 114, 116, 118
Jung, C. G., 115

Khan, Masud, 41, 59, 62, 63; on objects, 60, 61, 62; on dreams, 64, 65, 66, 67
"Kiss, The" (Chekhov), 100
Kissing, 5, 93–100
Klein, Melanie, 33, 37–38, 48, 59, 102, 103, 105, 107; on hate, 24; on love, 35–36; on depression, 36, 37; on instinct, 67; emotional development theory, 68, 75; paranoid-schizoid position, 75
Knowing, 4, 7, 108; beforehand, 15, 63; impossibility of, 60, 70; unknowing/not-knowing, 62, 63, 64, 65, 66, 107
Knowledge, 8, 9, 22, 23, 118; of self, 17, 67; object of, 24, 30, 64, 67; of sex, 117–118

Lacan, Jacques, 29, 121
Language, 2, 61, 109; of psychoanalysis, 4, 41, 44, 104; games, 8, 104; phobias and, 13, 16, 21; dreams and, 65; description of kissing, 95–96
Laplanche, Jean, 43, 76
Laughter, 9, 11. *See also* Jokes
Libido, 16, 117
Life-stories, 6, 103

Linking, 14, 19, 88–89, 92; risk/solitude, 32–33; solitude/attention, 40; parent/child, 49; link-envy, 127n9
Loss, 88, 89, 99
Love, 25, 33, 35–36, 53, 59–60, 85, 94, 110

Madness, 13
Magic/magical thinking, 25, 31, 71, 112
Mania, 53
Manic depression, 90
Masturbation, 9, 43, 50
McDougall, Joyce, 76
Meaning, 16, 21, 22, 76
Medicine, 2, 3
Melancholia, 71–72
Memory, 16, 17, 40, 57
Merging, 83, 89
Meyer, Eduard, 113
Michelangelo, 113, 114–115
Milner, Marion, 63
"Mind and Its Relation to the Psyche-Soma, The" (Winnicott), 44
Mind and mental life, 101; wishes and, 5, 54; states of, 14, 19, 106; development, 44, 45, 46, 88
Mirror, 99, 101; -stage, 125n6
Mitchell, Stephen, 34
Money-Kyrle, Roger, 22
Monotheism, 115–116, 119
Moods, 68, 70, 71, 78
Morality, 35, 124n11
Moses, 113, 114–115, 116, 118, 119, 120
Moses and Monotheism (Freud), 115–116
Moses of Michelangelo, The (Freud), 113
Mother(s), 47, 61, 69, 90–91; psychoanalyst as, 3, 102–103, 107–108; absence of, 27, 28–29, 32, 75–76, 91; caregiving by, 31, 32, 34, 44, 45; as object, 32, 38, 77, 104; relationship to infant or child, 32, 34, 35, 44–45, 61, 62, 71, 81, 89, 103, 105–106; separation from, 32, 35; desires or wishes of child and, 36, 45–46, 64; risk and, 41; mental development of infant and, 44–45;

desires of, 45–46; availability of, 63–64; as process of transformation, 77; fantasies of, 88, 91, 104, 108; phallic, 88; function of, 102, 103; role of, in psychoanalysis, 102–103, 106; maternal reverie, 105; pre-oedipal, 105, 106, 107, 108
Mothering, 44, 46, 59, 61, 102, 103–104
Mourning, 27, 71, 72. *See also* Death
Mourning and Melancholia (Freud), 71
Mouth: kissing, 5, 93–100; sucking, 93–94, 97, 98, 99
Murder, 89

Narcissism, 27, 99, 100
Narrative, 10
Need, 71
"Negation" (Freud), 24
Neurosis, 116
New Introductory Lectures, The (Freud), 5
Nietzsche, Friedrich, 33, 40
Nonappropriation, 126n22
Nourishment, 94, 97, 98, 99. *See also* Eating and feeding; Hunger
Nursing, 107. *See also* Breast
Nurture, 40, 60, 103

Object(s), 29, 40, 41; of fear and phobias, 15, 19, 21, 22, 25; sexual, 22, 31, 99; of knowledge, 24, 30, 64, 67; of love and hate, 25, 37, 38–39; -relations theory, 31, 49, 57, 58, 59, 62, 85, 89, 119; subjective, 31, 38, 39, 59–60, 124n17; maternal/paternal, 32, 38, 77, 104, 119; concern for, 33–34, 38, 39; disregard or destruction of, 37, 38–39, 76; of desire, 38–39, 62–63, 66, 76, 83, 88, 91; of worry, 49–50, 52; good, 60, 107; transitional, 60, 64, 89; transformational, 76–77; -seeking, 77; absence of, 78; obstacles and, 90; loss of, 99; visual, 104; of belief, 112, 121
Observation, 103–104, 105
"Observation of Infants in a Set Situation, The" (Winnicott), 72
Obsessions, 43, 53
Obstacles, 3, 59, 79–92

Oedipal relationships, 18, 48, 89. *See also* Pre-oedipal stage
Omnipotence, 29–30, 38, 39, 48, 50, 75, 80
Omniscience, 106, 107, 108
"On a Certain Blindness in Human Beings" (James), 15
"On Great and Little Things" (Hazlitt), 51
Orality, 93–94, 96, 97

Pain, 7–8, 10, 11, 50, 51, 53, 62, 119
Paradise Lost (Milton), 42
Paradox, 22, 23, 30, 33, 38, 43; of analysis, 48, 58, 105, 106, 121; of wishes, 68; linking, 89
Paranoia, 25
Paranoid-schizoid position, 75
Past, 2–3, 15, 16, 77, 110, 111
Pathology, 1, 32, 34, 41, 65, 71
Pedagogy, 104–105, 106
Penis, 6, 76, 88. *See also* Castration
Persecution, 26, 29, 51, 52, 54
Personality, splitting of, 94
Personalization process, 66, 67
Perversion(s), 32, 40, 43, 108; tickling as, 9, 11; contract, 38–39; objects and, 38–39, 62–63, 66; curiosity and, 63; sexual, 97
Philosophy, 5, 12
Phobia(s), 12–26, 53; agoraphobia, 13–16; opportunities for, 14–15; as transition, 14, 19; of children, 15, 27, 79–80; as defense, 15; claustrophobia, 17; object of, 19, 21, 22, 25; situation, 19, 21, 27–28; symptoms as, 22; defined, 25–26
Play, 11, 66
"Playing Mothers" (Phillips), 3
Pleasure, 9, 10, 11, 24, 25, 43, 50, 59, 119; sexual, 35, 97; obstacles to, 85; jokes and, 85–86
Pluralistic universe, 15
Poetry, 110
Pontalis, J.-B., 62
Possession, 59
Powers of Horror (Kristeva), 22
Pragmatism, 14
Preconceptions, 6

Pre-oedipal stage, 24, 75, 89, 102. *See also* Mother: pre-oedipal
Presence, 63
Present, 111
"Primitive races," 116, 117, 118
Privacy, 29, 49, 65
Projection, 16–17, 45, 76
Prostitution, 14
Protest, 76
Proust, Marcel, 16, 77, 86
Provocation, 19–20
Psyche, 86
Psychesoma, 44, 45, 46
"Psychoanalysis and Idolatry" (Phillips), 5
"Psychoanalysis and the Sense of Guilt" (Winnicott), 35
Psychology: The Briefer Course (James), 12
Psychopathy, 39
Punishment, 54
Purpose, 57
Pursuit, 52

"Question of Weltanschauung, The" (Freud), 5

Rage, 76, 79
Rank, Otto, 86
Rationality, 23. *See also* Irrationality
Reactivity, 23–24
Reality, 38, 55, 73, 119; external, 34, 89, 118; internal, 68, 89, 118
Recognition, 45, 46, 80, 82
Reconstruction, 65
Regression, 71
Religion, 5, 12, 111, 112–120
Remembering. *See* Memory
Reparation, 36–37, 38, 39
Repetition compulsion, 21, 59, 86–87
Representation, 57, 75
Repression, 85–86; of opportunity, 14–15; phobias and, 17; of states of mind, 19; unconscious and, 24; of solitude, 27; primary, 67; waiting and, 78; of experience, 87
Resistance, 86–87
Revenge, 9, 45, 114–115
Reverie, 105–106
Rilke, Rainer Maria, 40

Risk, 27, 29–30; of adolescence, 30, 31, 32; of adulthood, 30, 78; developmental, 38, 39; of solitude, 39
Romance, 3, 14, 95–96, 111
Rorty, Richard, 6
Roth, Philip, 52
Rousseau, Jean-Jacques, 84, 85
Ruskin, John, 42
Ruthlessness, 35–36, 37, 38, 39

Sachs, Hans, 109
Sadism, 45
Sadness, 47, 53
Sadomasochism, 5, 38–39, 44
Sartre, Jean-Paul, 30, 81–82
Satisfaction, 11, 59, 65, 84, 85; object of, 29; of self, 46, 99, 100; of infant, 66, 98, 99, 104; wish-fulfillment, 66, 67, 112; sexual, 98, 99; of desire, 100
Schreber case, 112
Science, 2, 3, 5, 7, 111, 112
Seduction, 46, 52, 106
Self, 59; identity of psychoanalyst, 5, 63, 105; identity of patient, 6, 8, 63, 105; -protection/-defense, 15, 16–17, 55, 98; -knowledge, 17, 67; versions of, 18, 19, 20; pathologizing, 22–23; loss of, 25; -trust, 29, 32, 41; -holding, 30, 32, 44, 46; relationship with, 34, 39–40, 94, 96; -confidence, 42, 73, 74; -cure, 42, 71; -presentation/ -expression, 43, 70, 73–74; -control, 44, 45, 114; isolation of, 46; -satisfaction, 46, 99, 100; worrying and, 54, 55, 57, 58; -doubt, 55, 58, 70; dreaming, 57, 64, 65, 67; -estrangement, 60; experience of, 62; -sufficiency, 69, 99; -transformation, 76–77; -destruction, 94; kissing of, 94, 98, 99, 100; disappointment with, 99; -esteem, 116. *See also* False Self; True Self
Sensuality, 10, 11, 116
Set situation, 72, 74
Setting: for phobias, 16; analytic, 29, 38, 61, 62–63, 72, 74, 101, 107, 109, 111; for development of guilt, 35; for desires, 64; for dreams, 64

Sexuality, 16, 22, 95, 96, 97, 100, 110; pleasure in hurting, 35; satisfaction in, 98, 99. *See also* Eroticism
Sleep, 28–29
Smirnoff, Victor, 87–88
Solitude, 27–41; in infants, 28, 29–30, 31, 41, 62, 64, 69, 75–76
Soma, 44, 48
Space, concept of, 66, 91
Splitting, 3–4, 94, 118
Still Life (Byatt), 52
Stories, 11, 43, 83, 95–96; psychoanalysis as, 4, 7–8; life-, 6, 103; phobias as, 23
Stroking, 10, 94
Studies on Hysteria (Freud), 1
Substitution, 75, 91, 94, 99, 100
Superstition, 112
Surprise, 9, 37, 44, 72, 90
Suzuki, D. T., 92
Swann's Way (Proust), 77
"Symbolism in Dreams" (Freud), 28
Symptoms, 1, 2, 29, 60, 112; use of, 13, 21; phobias as, 22–23, 79; patient's need for, 48, 119; worries as, 48, 49; as obstacles, 83–84

Table Talk (Hazlitt), 51
Taboos, 23
Technique/method, 2–3, 5, 101; estrangement, 22
Thanatos, 6
Theories: psychoanalytic, 3–4, 23–24, 61, 68, 87, 107, 112; of unconscious, 3, 6, 7, 15, 54, 65, 91–92; of sexuality, 10, 117; of phobias, 23; contradictory positions and, 88; sexual, 117, 118–119. *See also* Development/developmental theory
Thinking, secondary process, 92
Three Essays on the Theory of Sexuality (Freud), 10, 94, 97–98
Thumb sucking, 93, 94
Tickling, 5, 9–12
Time, 13, 40, 48, 75, 91, 92, 108
Timing, 104
Tradition, 3, 33, 50, 100
Transactions, 49
Transference, 21, 31, 32, 40, 74, 105, 108, 114; in analysis, 66, 101–102,

Transference *(cont.)*
103; negative, 70; interpretation
of, 106; open, 107; idolatry and,
115, 120
Transformation, 76–77
Transition/transitional phenomena,
12, 66, 72, 89; phobias as, 14, 19.
See also Object(s): transitional
Trauma, 11, 42, 43, 46, 87, 94, 100
Troilus and Cressida (Shakespeare), 97
True Belief, 111, 112, 118
True Self, 46, 50, 64, 107
Trust, 29, 32, 41
Truth, 5, 14, 15, 67, 118–119

Unconscious, 8, 41, 43, 120, 128n4;
Freudian theory of, 3, 6, 7, 15, 54,
65, 91–92; phobias and, 15, 22;
repression of, 24; defined, 25;
dreams and, 28, 57, 65, 66, 102;
wishes and desires, 54, 71, 83; fantasies, 59; obstacles and, 91–92;
communication, 101
Unhappiness, 112
Unpleasure, 24
Use: of analogy, 1–3, 4, 5, 51, 87; of
psychoanalysis, 1, 6, 65; of
instincts, 13; of symptoms, 13, 21;
of worries, 49–50; of objects, 59; of
dreams, 61, 64, 65, 104; of language, 61; of transference, 66; of
environment, 74

"Use and Abuse of Dream in Psychic
Experience, The" (Kahn), 64, 66

Waiting, 68–69, 72, 75, 76, 77–78
Wednesday Psychological Society, 109
Weil, Simone, 90
Winch, Peter, 90
Winnicott, D. W., 28, 49, 106;
holding concept, 29, 44, 59, 105,
107; on isolation and solitude, 31,
41; developmental theory, 33–35,
37–38, 39, 46, 59, 68; on False and
True Self, 34, 46, 60, 107; on
ruthlessness, 35–36; on objects, 39,
59, 60, 89; on composure, 44;
mother-infant relationship model,
61, 62, 66, 102, 103; on perversion,
63; on boredom, 72–74, 75
Wisdom, John, 67
Wish(es), 5, 7, 36, 95, 120; for
solitude, 40–41; to be understood,
46; -fulfillment/satisfaction, 54, 56,
66, 67, 112, 119; instinctual, 54, 55;
punishment for, 54; fantasies and,
59, 107; desire and, 68, 91; for
obstacles, 83, 91
Wittgenstein, Ludwig, 58
Worrying, 47–58
Writing, 33–34, 68; of psychoanalysis,
6, 7, 103, 106

Zweig, Stephan, 111